RAIZY FRIED

Published by:

RAIZY FRIED PUBLISHING

Lakewood, NJ 08701

www.raizyfried.com

Distributed by:

NIGUN DISTRIBUTION

4116 13th ave

Brooklyn NY 11219

718-977-5700

www.nigunmusic.com

We welcome all questions and comments

Raizy@raizyscookin.com

Written & Styled by: Raizy Fried

Photography by: Eluzer Friedman

Graphic Design and Layout by: Michelle Mozes

ISBN - 978-1-7923-4896-9

First Edition: November 2020

לכבוד שבת קודש

I thank the
Ribono Shel Olam for
everything He has given me:
For the appreciation.
The talent.
And for sending the right
people my way.

RAIZY FRIED

CHAPTERS

RECItPES

Hi,
I'm Raizy Fried.

I live in Lakewood and grew up in Boro Park, in Brooklyn, New York. When I attended Bnos Belz School, I was actually called by my full name, Chaya Raizy —which I never really liked. Why? Because when they called me Chaya Raizy, it sounded like one word—"Chareizy"—which sounded a lot like "Chareidi." Although I'm very proud of being a *chareidi* Chassidishe Jewish woman, I didn't appreciate being called that! Some friends said "Chareizy" so quickly, it literally sounded like *chrein*, which is Yiddish for horseradish. I don't particularly like chrein, and even if I loved horseradish and ate it three times a day, I still think that name would bother me. But my family always called me Raizy. *Baruch Hashem!*

We spoke mostly Yiddish at home—a real Yiddish! Words that even my Yiddish-speaking friends didn't understand were part of our language.

My childhood mornings smelled of אייער שפייז (scrambled eggs), fresh vegetables and dippity-do gel freshly combed into my brothers' curly *payos* (side locks). I came home from school to the aroma of supper simmering on the stovetop in our narrow white glossy formica kitchen on 43rd Street. Goulash, פאלשע לעיבער (mock liver),

פאשירט (fried ground chicken patties) were all frequent dinners, but איבערגעצויגענע פלייש (fried schnitzel), with fluffy mashed potatoes and corn, was by far our favorite, and always evoked squeals of joy!

Although our kitchen wasn't big, and I hardly cooked a thing before I was out of the house and married, that was where my siblings and I loved spending our time. I would chat with my mother as she sautéed onions, because almost every good Hungarian dish begins with a couple of sautéed onions.

No matter what type of kitchen one grows up in, you'll agree that kitchens are cozy. Kitchens are the hub of the home, where all of our senses come alive: sight, smell, taste and sound. Chassidishe music was the soundtrack of my childhood, playing from our stereo system on top of the white

All proud of the Melava Malka table I set on my own!

refrigerator. To this day, the heartfelt tunes of Belz and Moshe Goldman make me feel all warm and fuzzy, bringing me right back to my innocent childhood. In fact, the one thing that's missing from the experience conveyed through this lifestyle book is the background music! (For a moment there, I considered including a mechanism in the book that plays the coordinating music—like those musical birthday cards my grandmother got me, back in the day.)

Music is the language of my soul. It's what inspires me, keeps me going, calms me and touches my heart like nothing else can. You'll find me crying, davening and writing with music.

I'm actually listening to *Malachei Rachamim*, from the *Mesikus 2* album, as I write this. I play the keyboard, and I appreciate a vast selection of genres in music, but it's the heartfelt Chassidishe music that gets me every time, drilling right into the truth of who I really am.

You'll hear my children singing old songs like *Modeh Ani* from *Mesikus 2*, because it's constantly playing in the car, and *Hamalach Hagoel* from *Mesikus 1*, because that's what I sing at bedtime.

My children are growing up faster than I thought! It seems like just yesterday when I was yearning for each one of them. My family, my dear husband and children, fill me with deep gratitude that melts away any worries I may have. They remind me of the times I prayed for all the things I have now.

I believe my deep appreciation for the good things in my life is a result of the work I invested in being able to truly feel it. I didn't always appreciate what I was granted at birth, such as my talents and the way my mind thinks and works. I'm a very creative and out-of-the-box thinker. Today, I realize it's a true gift from Hashem, but it didn't always serve me well growing up. I used to hate the way my mind worked, because as a young girl among like-minded individuals, thinking differently made my life complicated. I remember crying myself to sleep almost every night, wishing I wasn't such a deep thinker!

But Hashem was very kind to me. He gave me parents who treated me with grace, supported me and provided me with creative outlets whenever they could. When the time came, they listened—really listened—to everything I wanted in a partner, and looked for a husband who was right for me. I got engaged after a traditional *beshow* (sit-in date) at the end of twelfth grade, and married my husband the following November.

I remember shopping with my great-grandmother from Belgium, may she rest in peace, while I was engaged. She asked me if I loved my *chassan*. Like most *kallahs* (brides), I was in the clouds, and said, "Of course!" I remember exactly where I was standing when she dismissed my words with a wave of her hand.

First you—"קודם דארף מען עסן א קילא זאלץ צוזאמען, נאכדעם קען מען וויסען אויב מען האט זיך ליב" have to eat a kilo of salt together, and then you can know if you like each other." I remember how confused I was, and how I kept replaying her words in my mind, trying to understand why she would dismiss my joy like that. אוי, איז זי אבער געווען גערעכט—oh, how right she was. And oh, how I miss her!

It's thanks to my husband that I'm where I am today. He always trusted and supported me. He stood by my side in the hardest of times.

Today, I'm very connected to myself and to my Creator. I know the whys, and when I don't, I buy a book or a *sefer* and learn until I understand.

Today, I live a truly fulfilling creative life. Today, my thoughts, my sensitivities and my experiences are cultivated into works of art. I write on a variety of subjects, and I'm a lifestyle blogger on Instagram, creating multimedia content that reflects my joy of cooking and homemaking.

This book is a tribute to my dear mother, a *balabusta* in her own right, my grandmother, and the diverse group of awe-inspiring Chassidishe women I grew up admiring. These women valued generosity and were always quick with a warm smile and a warm meal.

I was raised knowing that finding pleasure at home, in homemaking, is a gift that gives us the strength to go out into the world and do incredible things. And I believe that if we can find pleasure in cooking for our loved ones, in preparing our homes for Shabbos, and keeping our homes tidy, we are truly fortunate.

I love all the preparations for Shabbos. I love shopping for the food and the flowers, and turning on my favorite Shabbos songs as I peel and cook. I love baking challah. I love when the house is perfect and the floors are gleaming. From cooking, cleaning, setting the table, to doing my makeup in honor of Shabbos and donning the pearls around my neck ... as the Shabbos gets closer each week, the trepidation and joy escalates in my preparations, and my soul prepares to take flight. It's a form of art I use to express the deep emotions of love and gratitude that stir my soul.

This book will give you a glimpse of the rich heritage that brings me so much pride. I was raised knowing that we honor the holy Shabbos with the best! Both my husband and I grew up in true Hungarian-Chassidishe homes, where the Shabbos was glorified, as it should be. The words *Lekovod Shabbos Kodesh* echoed through both of our childhoods. I have such wonderful memories of my father coming home with bags of goodies on Erev Shabbos. Whenever my father picked out the finest fruit, or bought a nice bottle of wine, a new dish, or a new piece of silver for the Shabbos table, he would present it to us with radiant joy and the announcement, *"Lekovod Shabbos Kodesh!"* He would also constantly remind us (and still does) that Shabbos is the source of *bracha*, and there is great reward in spending money for the honor of Shabbos.

We put in a lot of effort to honor the Shabbos Queen and fill our home with that special Shabbos ambiance. We (my husband and I) truly believe that when it comes to honoring Shabbos, there is no need to worry about the cost. The Talmud *(Beitzah 16a)* states that when Hashem assigns a person's livelihood on Rosh Hashanah for the coming year, his Shabbos and Yom Tov expenses are not taken into account. The money spent in honor and celebration of Shabbos and Yom Tov will be repaid by the Almighty. Therefore, one should not hesitate to purchase the finest delicacies and clothing for Shabbos and Yom Tov; he should trust that these funds will be repaid to him in full. Whenever we are the lucky recipient of any goodness, from receiving a good job to the birth of another child (and everything in between)—we simply see it as the "rewards check" sent our way, as promised.

I'll show you my home and how I host the Shabbos Queen. You'll see how easy it is for you to bring a little of this *heimishkeit* into your home, no matter who you are and where you live.

I'll share tips and tricks along with the favorite recipes we keep making again and again. I'll tell you what keeps me connected and inspired when I get weary and the going gets rough. It is my wish that you connect to something in this book that you can use to improve your own Shabbos experience.

I hope you are sitting somewhere comfortable, so you can curl up and enjoy this book!

From one homemaker to another, *with love.*

Raizy

לכבוד שבת קודש

Cooking for Shabbos with Simcha and Love

Reb Mendel of Riminov said that the greatest blessings of the world come down from Heaven on Shabbos. If we want to be influenced by this tremendous blessing, we must accept it with words. Chazal tell us, "*Zachor* and *shamor* were said with a single statement" *(Rosh Hashanah 27a)*, hinting to the precious power of speech. We should therefore say the words "*Lekovod Shabbos Kodesh*" before eating the food at the Shabbos meal. *(Ateres Menachem 39)*

Our words have immense power. I try to remember to recite the words *Lekovod Shabbos Kodesh* as I purchase food and pretty things for the Shabbos table, when I cook the food and set the table. Saying these words every time you prepare something for Shabbos elevates the deed, along with the physical object or food. This brings much blessing to our homes and enhance the Shabbos experience.

The holy Chassidishe Rebbe, Harav Pinchas Kuritzer, commented on the statement regarding Sarah Imeinu that a blessing was found in her dough. This does not mean that Sarah had a small, blessed piece of dough that grew and multiplied. Avraham Avinu was affluent, and certainly had enough flour. The blessing was that the dough rose very well, baked to perfection. The challahs looked beautiful and were tasty.

Harav Pinchas Kuritzur added: A woman is referred to as *lechem*, bread (Rashi *Bereishis 39:6)*. For the challah to be successful—to rise and bake well, look pretty and shiny—it all depends on the woman of the home. When she is in a good mood, baking the challah with *simcha*, the challah will rise high, be fluffy and look beautiful. If the woman is preparing the challah with a sour face—the challah will reflect that!

אויב איז די פרוי בשעת'ן אנגרייטן מיט א זויער פנים, דעמאלט האבן די חלות אויך נישט קיין פנים.

(אמרי פנחת אות ל')

Music always puts me in a good mood, so I always turn on happy music while cooking for Shabbos. It helps me relax and enjoy the process. I often play Shabbos music, including *zemiros* and songs about Shabbos. Listening to Shabbos *zemiros* puts me in the right state of mind, so I can cook with heart and soul!

Entering Shabbos Like a Queen

Many women feel the desire to make Shabbos special. They prepare and work and cook up a storm. And instead of enjoying the fruits of their labor, they are so exhausted when Shabbos arrives that they can hardly keep their eyes open—forget about enjoying it!

This was me for many years. I thrived on that rush. I felt so accomplished as I did it all—the constant hosting, the weekly homemade baking, the full freezer, the perfectly ironed linen. I was idealistic and *geshikt*. I had the Bundt cake on the counter with the glaze dripping down, I sewed my own headbands and styled my own *sheitlach*.

By nature, I'm an overachiever and soul searcher. I was constantly trying to be the best version of myself, consumed by the need to accomplish and produce.

I remember trying to sew cute outfits for my children, a skill I dreamed of adding to my repertoire, but never perfectly mastered. After redoing the pants twice and getting it wrong again, I was all flustered, feeling like a failure. I cried on the phone to my mother, trying to figure out why I couldn't sew it right (of course, I was doing it without a pattern).

"You know what, Raizy?" my mother said. "You don't have to know how to do everything!"

But I didn't get it.

I had this vibrant vision of handmade matching outfits for my two babies, posing in a park for a photo shoot. The vision kept driving me.

I used to achieve perfection by avoiding life's most crucial relationship: the friendship between me and myself. I focused on the things that fueled me—making me feel accomplished. I pursued the thrill and rush of the sky-high standards I imposed on myself. I was driven by running the "Geshikt Balabusta Race."

When I felt the guilt creeping up, when I heard the "I should know better" voices emerging from within the shadowed folds of my brain, I turned up the volume of my life to block them out. I organized another closet. I popped another cake into the oven. I rewrote my schedules and lists so they'd appear neater. I invited more and more guests. I cleaned the cracks of my cordless phone, removing every ounce of residue with toothpicks around the dial keys. I filled my day with things to do, a drug that made me feel so much better. I whipped up a batch of cookies for a *simcha*; I scrubbed the pots; I filled the freezer; I crossed off another item from my to-do list. Ah … that always uplifted me. It felt heartwarming, like I was being enveloped in a long, tight hug.

I'm ambitious by nature. I always strived to be a better person, though I didn't always know how to achieve that. Back then, being a better person translated into doing more. I was very strong minded about what a devoted wife must do. I knew good mothers bend over backward for their children. Close friends offer help and over-extend themselves. Caring family members never miss a *simcha* and send over homemade delicacies at every occasion.

I considered myself fortunate; goodwill and problem solving came naturally to me. Because I sincerely cared and really liked helping others, the rat race of life wasn't even that exhausting. But here's where the problem came up.

לכבוד שבת קודש

So many of us women were raised with the mindset: "To be a good woman is to be good to others." If you're a good mother to your children, a good wife to your husband, a good friend to your friend, then you are good. While acts of kindness are always admirable, too many of us live with the misconception that our value and identity are inherently tied to the things we do for others.

We look up to the women who do it all! The woman who makes four different types of fish every Shabbos, a different recipe that each child particularly loves—she's the better mother.

Right?

This misconception feeds the horrible built-in heckler that tells us we didn't do enough, or we're not enough, or leads us to dismiss our accomplishments with, "It's nothing!" It's the same faulty mechanism in our brains that makes us incapable of accepting and appreciating compliments.

I find that many women, particularly of Hungarian descent, pride themselves on the way they model exemplary homemaking and generous hospitality. We live by the golden rules of etiquette; we host and treat everyone the way we want to be treated. Many women I know display a combination of beauty and strength. They are delicate and ornamental on the outside, while strong and fiery on the inside. These are women who always look elegant and put-together, are quick with a warm smile, a warm meal, and are simultaneously the undisputed leaders at their place of business and in their homes.

I give tribute to these women I grew up admiring. Yet while I appreciate the glamour and commend the generosity, I've *baruch Hashem* come to recognize that the grace and the fire, the goodwill and the martyrdom—they come at a cost. I've gained the awareness that striving to be that ultimate *balabusta* often feeds into the idea that you need to show up for other people in order to be of value.

I remember those low self-esteem days like it was today. I'll share one scenario that would repeat itself in different ways.

My mother-in-law is a great cook. She makes a large selection of dips each week for Shabbos. When I got married, I kept hearing how everything at my husband's home was homemade for Shabbos, including all the dips. I heard how nothing beats homemade dips, and that homemade dips are the best. Naturally, I wanted to be and serve only the best, which meant I made homemade dips every week. I felt a bit guilty for only making two or three dips a week, compared to my mother-in-law's five-plus weekly dips. But told myself I could only do what I can do, and at least the weekly tomato dip, olive dip and babaganoush were *heimish* and tasty.

What happened during those hectic weeks when a million things came up and I just couldn't make it? When the baby was up, night after night, and I felt like a zombie? What happened when I served store-bought dips for Shabbos?

I'll never forget how my cheeks burned as I sat at my husband's side at those Shabbos meals. I would feel terrible guilt that my husband could not experience his ultimate *Oneg Shabbos* because I couldn't push myself a bit harder to get my act together. There were so many emotions bubbling inside me, I couldn't even pinpoint what I was feeling. I would watch him dunk his challah into the store-bought tomato dip and see his unhappiness—even though it wasn't there. If he wasn't in the mood for tomato dip that week, and chose not to eat it—oh, my! The guilt would literally choke me.

Forget about enjoying the Shabbos food or the Shabbos meal. I sat feeling like I had betrayed my husband, battling with the voices in my head that berated me: "C'mon, you really couldn't do it? How hard is it to blend a few dips together?" I was a wreck. I would eat myself up with guilt throughout the entire meal.

In fact, my husband was fine with the store bought dip. Yes, he likes homemade food, but what he likes more is a calm and happy wife. He is a human being who understands that life happens, and I can't always do everything. He didn't even care.

But I was too messed up to notice any of that.

Instead, I took note of my feelings, promising myself that I would never again take the shortcut that made me feel so worthless. I would rather wash out the food processor a few times and push myself a bit more to avoid experiencing that shame and torture.

That's the kind of life I lived. I remember the rawness of those insecurities. I know I

12　　　　　　　　　　　　לכבוד שבת קודש

was always confident, but having confidence doesn't mean you have good self-esteem, and having low self-esteem is extremely painful. It makes you do crazy things and constantly push yourself so you can feel good about your work and yourself. Low self-esteem doesn't let you enjoy the precious things and moments in life. It makes every compliment sound like sarcasm.

Low self-esteem creates martyrs who keep striving to feel good about themselves. Martyrs can seem like nice, giving people, but they are really suffering inside. At a certain point, they get resentful and lash out at the people who are closest to them. Why? Not because the other person did anything wrong, but because she is feeling bad about herself.

A good friend once told me that there is something they forget to teach us in kallah classes—the most important skill is to take care of your emotions. "Your husband would rather eat chicken and potatoes for dinner and have a calm, available wife."

I love homemade dips. I agree with my in-laws that there's nothing else like it, and you'll find my favorite dip recipes in this book. But today, after much inner work, I also know the feeling of living. The feeling of contentment. And I know there's nothing like a wife and mother who is at peace with herself and has a deep sense of awareness of what she feels up to accomplishing—and where she needs to draw the line.

Over time, I've realized that giving and doing is only commendable when it comes from a healthy mindset and a genuinely happy heart. I've yet to find a martyr who isn't a smidgen resentful or bitter. It's something martyrs won't admit to anyone, not even to themselves. Because as soon as they feel the bitterness creep up, they quickly close the "feelings file" and run back to their place of comfort—their plans and mental to-do lists. They would rather clean all the crevices with toothpicks and scrub the white molding until it glows. Why? Because as exhausting as that work is, it's easier than facing the truth. People-pleasing and running away from yourself to attain materialistic perfection is so much easier than facing yourself and dealing with all those turbulent thoughts and emotions.

I've created a new class for myself. It's called "Hungarian and Chilled." Being Hungarian and chilled isn't an oxymoron; it's the phenomenon of snatching the best of both worlds. I believe you can be at once tough, kind and beautiful. I hold on tightly to the beautiful European etiquette I was raised with. I try to maintain exquisite poise, but only when it's realistic. I can make you feel infinitely welcome, but also let you know when you've pushed too far. I can be impeccably mannered and still enjoy a joyful mess created by my precious children. I can cook up a storm for Shabbos, and I can also buy Shabbos food and not feel guilty about it.

I can now fully enjoy being that *geshikt* Hungarian *balabusta*. I love the creating, the cooking, and serving up homemade delicacies on fine china, because whatever I do, I check in first with myself to make sure I feel up to it. I don't push myself; I respect myself. I try very hard not to call myself lazy when I'm simply exhausted. I now feel proud and deserving of the ultimate eishes chayil medal, even when we have store-bought challah for one month straight.

That said, this isn't that type of self-help book. I'm a very deep thinker, I've come a long way ... but I also love cooking delicious food and creating pretty things. Still, I believe it was necessary to tell you all this, so as you gaze at the "ideal," you remember to be human. You know how important it is to take care of your emotional health and always check in with yourself. Beautiful things are only beautiful when they come from a place of inner peace and emotional wellbeing.

This book is full of all the fine things and elaborate elegance I love, but you'll also find plenty of shortcuts and solutions to combat unrealistic expectations. With all the practical tips in the world, the most important foundation is your core belief in yourself.

True self-love is freeing! The new mindset I've cultivated made me realize that contrary to my old beliefs, my loved ones haven't been sticking around for my babka with streusel crumbs. They are here because they love me. And with that mindset, I'm able to enter Shabbos feeling like a queen!

לכבוד שבת קודש

How to Be a Queen

*Here are some tips to help you become the true
superwoman you need in your life.*

🌹 ACCEPT HELP

Stop alienating yourself from the people who love you and want to help you. Accept help from your spouse, or hire cleaning help. So many women have people offering them help, but they wave them off with, "Nah, I'm good," to prove to the world that they've got it all under control. Accepting help is a sign of strength.

🌹 GIVE YOURSELF LOVE

Self-care isn't about $200 massages, lush bath bombs, and face masks. Sometimes it's going to bed at 8 p.m. or letting go of a bad friend. Sometimes it's serving omelets for dinner or choosing not to attend a cousin's vort. It's forgiving yourself for not meeting your impossible standards and understanding you're worth it.

So many women keep pushing themselves with just another kugel, another dip and a batch of cookies, until it all gets to be completely overwhelming. Stop saying things like, "How long does it take to put up a pot of this or that?"

The core of self-care is not overdoing it, knowing when you've reached your limit. Not pushing yourself. It's not honorable to be a martyr! A burned-out, over-exhausted, depleted human has very little left to give. You can't pour from an empty vessel.

No matter how far I've come, it's still a frequent battle between what I want to do and what I can't do. I'm not always taking pink bubble baths, and my house isn't always as sparkling clean as the photos in this book. If you're reading this—you're human! You and I, we are both human. We will keep struggling with balance and stress management on one level or another. We must remember that we can't afford to abuse and overdrive our minds or bodies.

As my friend Ruth always says, "If you take care of your body when it whispers, you won't have to hear it scream."

🌹 GIVE YOURSELF TIME

Especially on Erev Shabbos, at the end of a long week, I find it crucial to infuse a portion of personal time into my day. Designate at least 30 minutes on Thursday or Friday to relax and do something nice just for yourself.

Some women like to relax and unwind before they begin cooking and cleaning the house for Shabbos. When I do this, I find I can start my cooking in a relaxed state and positive frame of mind.

Another possibility is to give yourself time after everything is done. Inserting your special self-care time after your Shabbos food is ready or when your house is clean gives you a great incentive, something to look forward to (in addition to Shabbos, of course). It's nice to sit down Thursday night with a nice cup of wine, a fresh slice of kugel, or a warm cup of tea.

My ultimate goal is to finish cooking everything on Thursday night, even if I finish late. I then have more time on Friday when I treat myself to a relaxed morning, a little shopping trip, a nice nap—whatever suits my mood.

Here are some ideas to rejuvenate yourself.

🌹 MOVE

Choose what you enjoy: yoga, Zumba, cardio or just dance! Try a power walk with a good friend or by yourself, plugged into some feel-good music, an inspiring podcast or shiur.

🌹 READ

I like to start this off with a day in the library, or browsing through a bookstore—there, that's another dose of self-care! Then curl up on the couch with a good book. Actually, though they always say to "curl up," you don't have to curl. You can also enjoy a good book lying down or sitting straight. I tried it and it works. Trust me!

🌹 EAT

Whip up your favorite meal just for yourself. Eat it alone, or order in!

🌹 BATHE

A warm bubbly bath. Personally, I enjoy being alone with my thoughts in the bath, without books, devices, or any entertainment. Supposedly many people like to read in the bath, though I still haven't figured out how this is done without getting the pages wet. If you can do it, go for it! In the worst-case scenario, your book will get sopping wet, and all the pages will form into one harmonious cluster.

❀ NATURE

Take a walk, or just sit there and enjoy the fresh air.

❀ FRIENDS

Go out with friends for a date. Enjoy some coffee and try to get in a few belly laughs.

❀ HOBBY

Do something you love! Paint, write, do puzzles…

❀ JUST GET OUT

When your husband gets home, you can make it your business to go out for "*maariv*" too. Spend a half hour outside to air out.

❀ RETAIL THERAPY

Buy yourself something nice. From personal experience, retail therapy is a thrilling rush that doesn't last, so don't make it expensive. Go to the dollar store, or get a nice new shade of lipstick at CVS.

❀ SLEEP

Try for an early bedtime. You'll feel like a new person the next day! Or allow yourself the luxury of a nap in the middle of the day.

❀ DATE NIGHT

Nothing feels better than reconnecting to your spouse or loved one.

Do something you enjoy for at least thirty minutes: whatever relaxes you and will make you feel like a lady. Please don't keep running in circles—because if you don't make it your business to take those precious minutes for yourself, to stop and inhale the fresh air around you, you'll keep buzzing around and around, from the pots to the hamper to the kids in the bath and then back to the pots … until Shabbos arrives, and you'll find yourself collapsed on the couch, feeling like that old, once white, now gray shirt that was cut into *shmattes*.

Giving yourself permission to pause and rejuvenate means the people in your life will get the best of you, rather than what's left of you.

🌸 KNOW YOU'RE ENOUGH

An emotionally healthy person feels valuable and content—even on days when she didn't accomplish anything. Keep telling yourself, "My value is in me. It has absolutely nothing to do with what I do!" It doesn't matter if the Shabbos food is homemade or purchased, if the dishes are real china or pretty disposables. You are valuable either way!

Dear Sister,

The road to attaining true menuchas hanefesh (peace of mind) can be painful. Be sure to treat yourself kindly. Pick yourself up when you fall, without self-beratement. Wipe away those tears with love.

It will take time, but if you crave it, I promise—you will get there!

Love,

Raizy

Oneg Shabbos

Shabbos is Joy

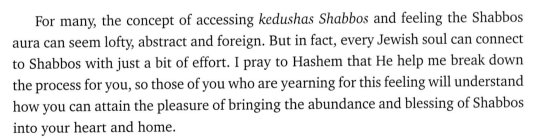

For many, the concept of accessing *kedushas Shabbos* and feeling the Shabbos aura can seem lofty, abstract and foreign. But in fact, every Jewish soul can connect to Shabbos with just a bit of effort. I pray to Hashem that He help me break down the process for you, so those of you who are yearning for this feeling will understand how you can attain the pleasure of bringing the abundance and blessing of Shabbos into your heart and home.

The Tur, in the beginning of the laws of Shabbos *(Orach Chaim 242)*, cites a number of passages from the Talmud that underscore the importance of not only observing but also sincerely enjoying Shabbos. Some examples:

One who observes Shabbos as a day of enjoyment and delight is rewarded with a "portion without boundaries," unlimited blessings. Just as he spent money freely for the purpose of honoring Shabbos, so is he rewarded with unlimited blessing.

Whoever observes Shabbos as a day of enjoyment and delight is granted all the wishes of his heart. Just as he enjoyed the Shabbos, so will Hashem grant him what he needs to always experience joy and contentment.

Shabbos actively invites delight in all the physical senses, as well as in the soul. It takes some ambition and action to intentionally create opportunities for *Oneg Shabbos*. This may sound lofty, but in practice it is so accessible and down-to-earth. A lot of spiritual work is physical, and *Oneg Shabbos* is the perfect example.

I am fortunate that this comes so naturally to me, for it's a part of my beautiful heritage. My parents and grandparents set beautiful Shabbos tables and made their homes sparkling clean and beautiful for *Oneg Shabbos*. Having gleaming floors, polished silver and a gorgeous table brought them joy. I have personally experienced it many times—when there is a week that I worked especially hard to bring in the Shabbos, I'll end up enjoying and feeling the *kedushas Shabbos* more.

Having fresh flowers around the house brings me immense joy. I used to buy one fresh bouquet of flowers each week for the dining room table. One week my husband brought home new flowers, and the bouquet from the previous week was still looking good and fresh. So I arranged the new flowers in the center of the Shabbos table, and placed the older bouquet in the kitchen. That Shabbos, whenever I walked into the kitchen and saw the flowers, I smiled. The blooms looked so pretty on our little oval-shaped kitchen table. They enhanced the whole kitchen. Even my husband noticed and commented about how special it made the kitchen feel.

That's when we decided we were going to make it a thing. We started buying two bouquets every week, a big one for the dining room and a smaller one for the kitchen table. It fills my home with beauty and my heart with joy. Having a pretty table brings me joy. Fresh flowers bring me joy. Of course, delicious food helps too!

I am constantly looking for different ways to enhance my *Oneg Shabbos*. A few years ago, I bought a beautiful *zemiros* book that has all the Yiddish lyrics to the songs I grew up with. Songs from Reb Yomtov Ehrlich, songs from the old *Lechaim*

לכבוד שבת קודש

tapes from Reb Yosef Moshe Kahane, songs we sang in camp … One activity that brings me a lot of pleasure is singing my favorite Yiddish songs from the *zemiros* book after candle lighting, or on Shabbos afternoon.

What brings YOU joy? Is it pretty things? Good food? Is it taking the time to make up your face beautifully for Shabbos and looking pretty? Taking the time to Daven? Chocolate? A good book? Will buying a new Shabbos robe bring you joy? Wine? A deep Shabbos nap?

Sit with yourself and think about it. Try different things, figure it out, because that's what you need to do for Shabbos. Make *Oneg Shabbos* part of your practice in whatever form makes sense for you.

Slowly, as you start investing time, money and effort in your Shabbos experience, you'll begin to notice how excited you are for Shabbos, how the Shabbos atmosphere turns warmer. The meals cozier. The ambiance loftier. The actions you've been doing for years become more meaningful. You'll feel a flutter, and then another … until you feel a warmth that overtakes your heart entirely. You'll feel your soul take flight, you'll feel the *kedushah*. You'll feel it all here, in your own home, in you. It will feel magical, but you'll know good and well that it's not magic. It's the result of effort with intention.

Setting the Shabbos Table

אתקינו סעודתא דמהימנותא שלמתא חדותא דמלכא קדישא

Prepare the feast of perfect faith, the joy of the Holy King.

The primary *kedushah* of Shabbos is achieved through the Shabbos meal. The Shabbos table is not merely a platform for food, dishes and drinks—it becomes "the table that is placed before Hashem." The Shabbos table is a triumphant welcome for the Shabbos Queen.

Our sages teach us that we eat the Shabbos meal in the nicest room in the home, to welcome the holy Shabbos in a suitable manner. My father-in-law says, *"Lekovod Shabbos Kodesh,"* every time he buys a new piece to enhance the décor of the dining room. Many people actually call the dining room the *Shabbos tzimmer* (Shabbos room). The Shabbos meal is served with the best that we own, the finest dinnerware.

When it comes to preparing for Shabbos, especially in the winter, I try not to leave any major tasks for Friday. I love setting the table on Thursday night—it fills my home with a sense of calm and anticipation.

The Art of Table Setting

A table is an empty space that you can transform into a wonderland of style and thoughtfulness. In my opinion, the art of table setting is not about pretty flowers or beautiful chargers and china. All of these together often form a pretty mess that can hurt the eyes and clutter the mind. The art lies in color coordination and most of all, balance! Big puffy peony napkin rings only look beautiful when paired with the right minimalistic centerpieces and china.

Napkins

FABRIC NAPKINS VS. PAPER NAPKINS

I appreciate the finer things in life, especially for Shabbos! I generally don't like using printed paper napkins on their own because I find them cheap-looking and flimsy. When I use paper napkins, I place it over a basic white fabric napkin. This takes it up a notch and makes it suitable to top fine china.

NAPKIN FOLDING

The placement of napkins can add a decorative flourish, especially when they are folded in beautiful ways, like a fan shape or a pretty bow.

For a pretty bow: Spread a dinner napkin out so it's lying flat. Fold the opposite sides in so they meet at the center. Then fold horizontally again at the center to form a narrow, ribbon-like shape. Next, fold the short ends in so they meet at the center. Cinch in the middle. Use a ribbon in a coordinating color or a napkin ring to hold it together.

I prefer the all-time classic: Fold the napkin over diagonally into a triangle. Cinch it at the center with a pretty napkin ring and fluff up the open top like a pretty bouquet.

NAPKIN RINGS

Over the years I've managed to collect quite a variety of different napkin rings.

I believe you can create really pretty napkin rings without breaking the bank. Here are two of my favorite ideas.

The easiest way to create beautiful napkin rings is by picking up nice faux florals at your local discounted gift shop or Michael's. Cut the stems off and use hot glue to attach them to hard plastic disposable napkin rings. You can pick up disposable napkin rings at Amazing Savings. They usually come in packages of six. And you don't have to stick with flowers—be creative!

Another idea is to use a plain velvet ribbon. Tied into a pretty bow, it is reusable and looks so elegant, especially when it matches the flowers.

TABLECLOTH

WHITE

We follow the age-old *minhag* of using a white tablecloth. There are many reasons for this custom. The primary reason is that white symbolizes purity. In the Beis Hamikdosh, when Hashem forgave all our sins, the red thread turned white. *Chazal* tell us (*Shabbos 118b*) that Hashem considers everyone who keeps His Shabbos as if they offered a grain offering in the Beis Hamikdash, and forgives their sins. Shabbos gives our souls redemption over all our troubles.

FABRIC VS. PLASTIC

One of the most frequent questions I get is how I can have my table set so early without my children throwing the glassware on the floor. This is followed by another popular question—how can we eat without plastic covering the fabric tablecloth? How do you prevent it from getting dirty, especially with young children?

Regarding spills and stains, I generally only use table linens that are washable and non-iron. I use a thicker white napkin as a placemat at the children's places, underneath the charger, after *Kiddush*. This helps protect the tablecloth at their settings.

Even if the tablecloth gets stained from spills—which definitely happens!—I prefer the beauty of a glistening textured fabric with a few stains over a perfectly clean tablecloth, with its true beauty concealed under plastic. But to each her own—do what works best for you.

Regarding the nature of children, I believe children are intuitive human beings who can be trained. I'm far from a parenting expert, but I can say this: teaching children care, etiquette and not to ruin the pretty things that other people worked hard on are all part of basic *chinuch*.

I believe if you have healthy children and a decent relationship with your children, if you have a loving connection, why would they want to upset you by ruining something pretty that you worked so hard to create?

I grew up with a beautifully set table *lekovod Shabbos* that was set every week on Thursday night. I grew up in a house full of children, some wilder than others. Never were we punished for spilling grape juice by mistake. I don't remember anyone minding the set table. We grew to appreciate it.

In general, I believe that life doesn't have to stop when there are little children in the house. Mommy is allowed to have hobbies. One of my greatest joys is setting the Shabbos table. For me, it's a labor of love. When children see the care and good taste involved in preparing the Shabbos table, they are essentially sensing and learning the *chashivus* of Shabbos—intuitively understanding that it is worthy of such honor.

Floral Design

There's a midrash that says that Hashem created flowers specifically to adorn our Shabbos tables. I use the type and color of the flowers to inspire the rest of my table décor. I might match up napkins or a napkin ring in the same color. According to the fresh picks of the week, I'll decide whether to go with gold, silver, or both. Yes, you can mix both!

I've picked up most of my floral tips and tricks from my weekly sessions in flower shops, picking out flowers and speaking to experienced florists.

Arranging Flowers

Sometimes I'll buy a ready bouquet and simply place it in a vase, which is beautiful. But when I have the time, I love making my own floral arrangements. Trimming and arranging these gorgeous natural gifts that we call flowers is truly therapeutic!

When arranging flowers, I try to keep the arrangement low. It's easy to hand things over it and it doesn't block the view, so you can converse with family members on the other side of the table.

To keep the flowers in place, which is particularly important for wide-mouthed vases, I never use floral sponges. Instead, I use the popular tape grid hack *(see page 32 for instructions)*. This works better because the flowers sit in more water, helping them stay fresh for longer.

KEEPING FLOWERS FRESH

Nothing is more disappointing than a beautiful bouquet of flowers dying before Shabbos. With proper care, your flowers should last. Here are a couple of tips to help prolong the life of your flowers.

CHOOSING FLOWERS

When choosing your flowers in the store, make sure every part of the bouquet is in good condition. Check that none of the leaves are withered or brown, or show signs of disease. The flowers should be either in a bud or slightly open, but feeling firm.

Unfortunately, depending on where you buy your flowers, they can be less than fresh when you get them. I suggest buying from a few different sources and see if you notice a consistent pattern. You'll usually find one purveyor who has fresher flowers than others.

I also make sure all the flowers are wet at the bottom and that they are all the way in the bucket when I pull them out! You can also tell how fresh a flower is by how springy the blossoms are. The older ones may be soft. You want firm! Closely examine the blooms that are not tight. Touch them gently to see if they feel soft or aren't springy to the touch. Those are the ones you should leave behind.

TRIMMING

When cut flowers have been left out of water for any length of time, cells start to form over the cut ends of the stems, which will prevent the stems from taking up water readily. To remove this sealed portion, snip off about one inch from the stem ends. A slanted cut allows a better intake of water. It's also helpful to remove any leaves that will be below the water level of the vase. Wet leaves will rot and taint the water.

לכבוד שבת קודש

Accents for Flowers

A pretty accent idea that I love: pearls adorning flowers. This goes particularly well with red or white roses. Use pins with white pearl heads and stick them into the center of a couple of roses. Watch how these little details can beautify a rose!

Tape Grid Instructions

- Add water to your vase.
- Use narrow white tape to form a grid across the opening. Make sure there's enough tape hanging over the sides, so the tape stays put.
- Strip leaves from the flower stems, then trim the stems to the proper length, proportionate with the vase.
- Arrange the flowers in the holes of the tape grid, making sure the flower heads hide the tape. Try not to get the tape too wet as you work.

ARRANGING

Gently lift each stem, shaking off excess water. Then arrange it in your vase.

Flowers that have woody stems, like roses and hydrangeas, last longest if you arrange them in a deep vase. Flowers with fleshy stems, like tulips and daffodils, will do better if the water level is lower, which prevents the stems from rotting. When arranging flowers, the shorter you cut the stem, the longer the flower will last, since the water will reach the head more easily.

FLOWER FOOD

Dissolve 3 tablespoons of sugar and 2 tablespoons of white vinegar per quart of warm water and fill the vase. When you fill the vase, make sure the cut stems are covered with 3–4 inches of prepared water. The sugar will nourish the flowers, while the vinegar will inhibit bacterial growth.

WATER CARE

Adding Clorox bleach to the flower vase water keeps flowers healthy. Clorox kills microorganisms, so your flowers last longer and the water doesn't get funky as fast. Using gloves, add ¼ teaspoon of Clorox bleach to every 1 quart of water and stir to mix.

Change the vase water regularly to make the flowers last longer, and renew the flower food when you do this. I change the water from the vases on Motzei Shabbos. I also snip the edges of the stems to prolong the life of the blooms, so they beautify my home all week long!

PLACEMENT

Avoid placing cut flowers in direct sunlight or near a source of heat. Sun and heat speed up the ageing process, which will make the flowers wilt and decay more quickly than in a cooler location.

HYDRANGEAS

Hydrangeas are pretty, but they suck up water! They need a little extra help to make them last longer. First, remove *all* leaves. Cut the stems on a slant. I also use my shears to cut a 2–3-inch diagonal slit in each stem to keep the stem open and allow the water to travel up the stems more easily! I cut two slits a couple of inches from the bottom of the stem to form a plus sign. Cut the stems short. The stems shouldn't be taller than the vase and the buds should lean comfortably on top of the ledge of the vase.

TULIPS

To keep tulips from wilting, add a penny to the vase. The copper will keep the stems straighter! (For clarification regarding *muktzeh* concerns, please ask your Rav for guidance.)

לכבוד שבת קודש

Shabbos & the Woman of the Home

אשת חיל מי ימצא, ורחק מפנינים מכרה

A woman of valor, who can find?
She is more precious than pearls.

Shabbos is an integral part of every Jewish family and a big chunk of our duties as *Yiddishe mammes* and homemakers. It's something we do every single week, 52 times a year! Cooking delicious Shabbos meals, preparing the house and lighting the Shabbos candles—all welcome the Shabbos ambiance into our homes. Setting this atmosphere and instilling the love of Shabbos into our children is our duty as Jewish mothers. When children grow up with fond memories of Shabbos, it's ultimately to our credit.

I know just how challenging it can be. I've got my own family to care for, *baruch Hashem*, and a job that keeps me really busy. Making Shabbos on a weekly basis can be very overwhelming. It all goes down at the end of the week, when we often find ourselves exhausted. Some weeks I sit there feeling so depleted, wondering how I'll gather the energy to do what must get done.

I know about those inner voices, and I would like to clarify something.

Just because it's been done for generation after generation by Jewish women, just because everyone does it every week, doesn't make it less difficult or special. I believe it is precisely because we do it every single week that we are an incredible nation of awe-inspiring women!

"A woman of valor, who can find? She is more precious than pearls … Grace is elusive and beauty is vain, but a woman who fears Hashem—she shall be praised. Give her credit for the fruit of her labors, and let her achievements praise her at the gates."

Eishes Chayil is sung at every Shabbos table throughout the world in praise of Jewish women everywhere. On the most basic level, it has become a way of expressing gratitude to the woman of the house. For what is a more fitting time to sing her praises than on Friday night, after she worked tirelessly to ensure that the Shabbos Queen is greeted in royal fashion?

There are many midrashim that claim that the Woman of Valor in the song does not refer to the generic, praiseworthy woman. *Eishes Chayil* refers to specific great women in Jewish history. Other commentators say this song is about the Shabbos Queen, about the Torah, or the *Shechinah* (G-d).

In truth, all the explanations are interconnected, for it is the noble woman of the home who makes it into a Divine spiritual place—a haven for Torah, a place where our souls can flourish and are able to serve Hashem.

לכבוד שבת קודש

Down to my core, I'm depleted and sore —
Have I got the strength,
To do it all again?
In exhaustion, I wallow and ponder
My thoughts — they wander...

Then I recognize the cause of my aches and pains.
Realization hits, and only gratitude remains.
My demanding kinderlach, my family,
My hard work — my talent and capability.
Suddenly I've been lifted — I'm floating in the skies.
Gone are my frustration and cries.

My sense of purpose burns like fire,
As my soul meets its Source, uniting in desire.

Tatte, although I know I have your love from before,
I want to please and honor you more
I want to do it all right,
Prepare my home for your warm Shabbos light.

Tatte, I give you my all. Filled with anticipation,
Awaiting candle lighting with peace and elation.
Yearning for that sacred time
When your caress of love swells this heart of mine...

חי'ו הכל מן הכל

A woman
of valor who can find? Her
price is far above pearls. The heart of her
husband safely trusts in her, and he has no lack
of gain. She does him good and not evil all the days of
her life. She seeks wool and flax, and works willingly with her
hands. She is like the merchant's ships; she brings her food from
afar. She rises while it is yet night, and gives food to her household, and
a portion to her maidens. She considers a field, and buys it; with the fruit
of her hands she plants a vineyard. She girds her loins with strength, and
makes strong her arms. She perceives that her merchandise is good; her lamp
is not extinguished at night. She lays her hands to the distaff, and her hands hold
the spindle. She stretches out her hand to the poor; she reaches forth her hands
to the needy. She is not afraid of the snow for her household, for all her household
are clothed with scarlet wool. She makes for herself coverlets; her clothing is fine
linen and purple. Her husband is known in the gates, when he sits among the
elders of the land. She makes linen garments and sells them, and delivers belts
to the merchant. Strength and dignity are her clothing, and she laughs at the
time to come. She opens her mouth with wisdom, and the law of kindness is
on her tongue. She anticipates the needs of her household, and the bread
of idleness, she does not eat. Her children rise and celebrate her; her
husband also, and he praises her: "Many daughters have done
valiantly, but you surpassed them all." Grace is deceitful,
and beauty is vain; but a woman who fears Hashem,
she shall be praised. Give her of the fruit of her
hands, and let her works praise her in
the gates.

אֵשֶׁת חַיִל מִי יִמְצָא

וְרָחֹק מִפְּנִינִים מִכְרָהּ. בָּטַח בָּהּ לֵב בַּעְלָהּ,
וְשָׁלָל לֹא יֶחְסָר. גְּמָלַתְהוּ טוֹב וְלֹא רָע, כֹּל
יְמֵי חַיֶּיהָ. דָּרְשָׁה צֶמֶר וּפִשְׁתִּים, וַתַּעַשׂ בְּחֵפֶץ כַּפֶּיהָ.
הָיְתָה כָּאֳנִיּוֹת סוֹחֵר, מִמֶּרְחָק תָּבִיא לַחְמָהּ. וַתָּקָם בְּעוֹד
לַיְלָה, וַתִּתֵּן טֶרֶף לְבֵיתָהּ וְחֹק לְנַעֲרֹתֶיהָ. זָמְמָה שָׂדֶה וַתִּקָּחֵהוּ,
מִפְּרִי כַפֶּיהָ נָטְעָה כָּרֶם. חָגְרָה בְעוֹז מָתְנֶיהָ, וַתְּאַמֵּץ זְרוֹעֹתֶיהָ.
טָעֲמָה כִּי טוֹב סַחְרָהּ, לֹא יִכְבֶּה בַלַּיְלָה נֵרָהּ. יָדֶיהָ שִׁלְּחָה בַכִּישׁוֹר,
וְכַפֶּיהָ תָּמְכוּ פָלֶךְ. כַּפָּהּ פָּרְשָׂה לֶעָנִי, וְיָדֶיהָ שִׁלְּחָה לָאֶבְיוֹן. לֹא
תִירָא לְבֵיתָהּ מִשָּׁלֶג, כִּי כָל בֵּיתָהּ לָבֻשׁ שָׁנִים. מַרְבַדִּים עָשְׂתָה לָּהּ,
שֵׁשׁ וְאַרְגָּמָן לְבוּשָׁהּ. נוֹדָע בַּשְּׁעָרִים בַּעְלָהּ, בְּשִׁבְתּוֹ עִם זִקְנֵי אָרֶץ.
סָדִין עָשְׂתָה וַתִּמְכֹּר, וַחֲגוֹר נָתְנָה לַכְּנַעֲנִי. עֹז וְהָדָר לְבוּשָׁהּ,
וַתִּשְׂחַק לְיוֹם אַחֲרוֹן. פִּיהָ פָּתְחָה בְחָכְמָה, וְתוֹרַת חֶסֶד עַל
לְשׁוֹנָהּ: צוֹפִיָּה הֲלִיכוֹת בֵּיתָהּ, וְלֶחֶם עַצְלוּת לֹא תֹאכֵל: קָמוּ
בָנֶיהָ וַיְאַשְּׁרוּהָ, בַּעְלָהּ וַיְהַלְלָהּ: רַבּוֹת בָּנוֹת עָשׂוּ חָיִל,
וְאַתְּ עָלִית עַל כֻּלָּנָה: שֶׁקֶר הַחֵן וְהֶבֶל הַיֹּפִי, אִשָּׁה
יִרְאַת ה' הִיא תִתְהַלָּל: תְּנוּ לָהּ מִפְּרִי יָדֶיהָ,
וִיהַלְלוּהָ בַשְּׁעָרִים מַעֲשֶׂיהָ.

Lighting the Shabbos Candles

As the sun begins to set in a brilliant combination of radiant hues, I give *tzedakah* and light the Shabbos candles. Bringing my hands over the flames toward me signifies that I'm drawing the spirituality and holiness of Shabbos into my home and my life. I cover my eyes, recite the *bracha*, and enter an affectionate embrace with my *Tatte in Himmel*. For those few moments, life stops as I reconnect. My heart open and raw, I stand talking to my Tatte in Yiddish. I request what's important to me, not measuring my words. I quiver as I unpack my heart like a little child.

I thank Him profusely, because my life is essentially good. All I've experienced and keep experiencing, all the challenges and traumas, have taught me just how good my life really is. Standing near the Shabbos flames, I feel an overwhelming sense of gratitude for everyone and everything wonderful in my life. Even the situations that are imperfect or unsolved feel somewhat lighter at those moments.

I also pray, asking Him for everything. Because no matter how good my life is, it's sometimes hard. Oh, so painfully hard. Watching and caring. Coping and living. Loving and thriving. Thinking and breathing.

I don't need to understand everything. I know I never truly will. But I also know that I need to be wise and pass the pain and worry onto broader shoulders. Our Father—He can and wants to help us carry the load. All we need to do is open up and release it all to Him.

I used to save these precious moments for the big things in life, but I've learned that to our Father in Heaven, there is no difference between big and small. It's all the same to Him; it's all effortless for Him. There's nothing that's too big or too minute. Nothing too silly to pray for. He is the Creator of every thought that's in my mind and every desire in my heart.

Every week, I pray for an uplifting and enjoyable Shabbos. I pray that this week's Shabbos should be *geshmak* in both *ruchniyus* and *gashmiyus*. For the children, that they get their attention, and for my husband and I, that we have enough of our own time. For the food to be tasty, for the ambiance to be heartwarming and for the table discussions to be enjoyable. For me, to relax and rejuvenate. For us all to enjoy every minute.

Most of all, I pray that I should feel the holiness of Shabbos in every bone, that it should overtake me in a euphoric, tangible way. It's this prayer that takes precedence every week.

As I welcome the Shabbos into my home, I feel its warmth overtaking my senses. Feelings that seem so natural, yet special. Emotions that are welcome, yet almost overwhelming. My essence is dancing through my heart and soul, engaging my physical senses. The most beautiful things in the world cannot be seen or even touched—they are felt with the heart.

I believe that the feelings and sensations of *kedushas Shabbos* come with labor. I believe that both my personal emotional inner work and the weekly physical Shabbos preparations play a big role in acquiring them.

However imperfect I am as a mother, I think I'm pretty good at setting the Shabbos atmosphere, at turning our home into a haven worthy of hosting the holy Shabbos Queen. I constantly give to my husband and children, yet I feel that this—creating the Shabbos atmosphere—is the most precious gift I could ever give them. I sometimes imagine what is to come. In a blink, these children of mine will no longer be living in our home. Soon it will be completely up to them. As tears roll from my eyes into the palms of my sweaty hands, I pray that they have the desire and the will for this task.

I'll sometimes watch them get dressed for Shabbos happily, with a spring in their step. Often, they curl up next to me on the couch, or lean on my shoulder at the Shabbos meal, which they don't usually do during the week. Do they feel what I'm feeling? When I remove my hands from my wet face after *licht bentching*, I look at my children's faces. They look so *lechtig* and refreshed, full of mystical light and radiant joy. Do they feel it? Do they understand that this special Shabbos coziness doesn't just appear out of thin air? Do they realize that honoring the Shabbos is a constant endeavor that readjusts as you grow … and that when you get to know yourself, it takes on a whole new level of meaning?

"… Make me worthy to raise learned children and grandchildren, who are wise and understanding, who love and fear Hashem, people of truth, holy and attached to Hashem, who will dazzle the world with Torah and goodness and service of Hashem. Please hear our prayers in the merit of our matriarchs Sarah, Rivkah, Rachel and Leah, and ensure that the glow of our lives will never be dimmed. Show us the glow of Your face …"

Motherhood is a miracle and an amazing gift. I pray that I never, ever take it for granted.

There will always be that part of me that aches for the loneliness and pain so many suffer, waiting for their miracle.

"Grant all those still waiting with the *zechus* to light additional candles of their own, and souls that will light up this world …"

RAIZY FRIED

These soul moments at candle lighting and the comforting Shabbos day that follows is such an inherent part of my life and who I am, that I naturally assume others experience the same special feeling. But do they? What is Shabbos to others? What does it really take to create that feeling?

Evoking the wellspring of the incredible Shabbos aura and blessing takes more than a few tasks and a checklist. It's an attitude that stems from the core of our individuality. It's the desire to bring the most essential parts of ourselves to the Shabbos table. We might not always feel like we have enough strength or natural warmth to ignite the Shabbos atmosphere. But if we know how to create warmth using what's inside us, we can search for it on the outside and bring it inside, no matter where we are in life.

לכבוד שבת קודש

The Little Things

In most homes, Shabbos feels special. This special feeling comes from preparing our best for Shabbos. But we don't have to get caught up in thinking that it takes a lot of effort to make Shabbos special for our children. More often, it is the details of our childhood, the little gestures of passion, that transform our experiences.

Some of my memories...

The towel my mother sometimes tossed in the dryer for me, to warm it for after my bath.

The floral paper napkin that was fluffed up lovingly and placed in the center of the Bundt cake, *lekovod* the *Cheder Firhen* or the *simcha.*

The little Rosh Chodesh treats.

The charming little ceramic tchotchkes that adorned the kitchen windowsill.

The embroidery and the monograms. The engraved words etched in the silver.

The potpourri and the tassels.

The jello my mother often made for birthday parties.

The warm sweet *bundash* (French toast), made of leftover challah and given with love in a paper towel for Sunday breakfast.

While I absolutely love the finer things in life and grandiose gestures, I try to remember that my coziest childhood memories aren't of the grand family trips we took (though there were plenty of those too), but from the little things:

The stories of the Baal Shem Tov and his *talmidim* that my father would tell every Motzei Shabbos at *Melava Malka*.

The little game we played where you *tzip* (pinch) each other's hands, piling our hands on top of each other, building a tower of hands while we chanted the Hungarian, "Csip, csip, csóka …" and then mashing up all our hands when the chant was over.

My mother's delicious little cream puffs.

The times my mother trusted me to set the table as a little girl—and I folded and styled those paper napkins.

The practical tips from the weekly *Oneg Shabbos* pamphlet, עס קען אייך צוונצקומען.

The Shabbos treats we would get each week. In particular, I remember the chocolate covered orange wafer bricks that came in a white bag in a blue box, and a cool product that was on the market for a while, a straw version of the popular La-Hit Chocolate—my father got them for us as a Shabbos treat. Cups of Shabbos morning milk sipped through those straws were something else!

Which reminds me of the licorice straws we created, and all the licorice we had to eat until we got one that allowed a smooth orange juice flow.

Did you notice how many of these little memories are of Shabbos?

I try to keep these memories alive so they continue to inspire me, as I strive to infuse the sweetness of Shabbos into my own home. It's easy to get blinded by the big, glittery stuff. It's easy to get upset when the vision doesn't pan out. If our kids don't participate at the Shabbos meal we worked so hard for, or don't behave as they should, it's easy to get lost in a battle for control.

But we are not in control of anyone but ourselves. As long as we do our part, they will grow up and love Shabbos, even if they might not seem to care much about it right now.

I vividly remember the Shabbos meals I spent away from the table as a teenager. I spent many Shabbos meals in my room doing super important things that couldn't wait, such as memorizing lyrics of songs from the little pamphlets that came with the CDs. (Remember how it was back in the day, when we got a physical booklet with all the information about the album?) *Baruch Hashem*, I still grew up with great, cozy Shabbos memories, and I think I turned out okay. Don't let these things get you down. It'll be fine. You just continue to do your part.

It's especially beautiful when preparing for Shabbos becomes a family project and you involve your children. I know families where the children each have a Shabbos job, like making the dips, or baking a cake, or making dessert. This infuses such *simcha* in the home—the children feel essential to bringing in the Shabbos atmosphere. Everyone is part of the buildup; everyone feels like she has a part in it.

Spending time with your children and giving them attention doesn't need to take a lot from you. Consider doing one special thing, like reading them a book every Shabbos, reviewing their parshah sheets, or just admiring their creations and stories. Find something that works for you and interests your children. There are families who take Shabbos walks, and that's the highlight of their Shabbos, I think that's so beautiful!

I try to be careful not to enter Shabbos completely drained, so I have the energy to enjoy this special day and fill it with little words, little songs, little hugs, little kisses, more little words, and little goodies for my loved ones.

Also, little naps. Just for myself.

The Shabbos Meal

אכול בשמחה כי כבר רצך

ברוב מטעמים ורוח נדיבה יזכו לרב טוב המתענגים בה

Eat in gladness, for He has already shown you favor ... with abundant delicacies and a generous spirit ... They will merit much good, those who take pleasure in the Shabbos!

(Verse from the song מנוחה שמחה traditionally sung on Friday night.)

Everything one eats on Shabbos becomes purely spiritual. Although one usually eats more than he needs on Shabbos, the *gashmiyus* becomes *ruchniyus*. Harav Hakodesh from Slonim states that through eating on Shabbos, a person can have a greater *aliyah*—transcend to a higher spiritual level—than through prayer. *(Toras Avos L'Shabbos)*

Our sages tell us that we should prepare a cooked dish for Shabbos that is rich, and a drink that is pleasurable—everyone according to his budget. Someone who spends more on Shabbos to prepare good food is praised. Eating meat and drinking wine is an *Oneg Shabbos. (Rambam Hilchos Shabbos 30)*

The Gemara *(Shabbos 118)* says that whoever takes pleasure in the Shabbos, Hashem will fulfill all his requests. The Yismach Yisrael says that the food of Shabbos has the same holiness as the food from the *korbanos* in the Beis Hamikdosh.

There are many beautiful ideas mentioned by our Gedolim regarding the Shabbos food. It enables positive spiritual influences to flow into our lives, it strengthens our *yiras Shomayim*, it brings about physical healing—and many more blessings for Hashem's beloved Jewish children.

TRADITIONS

While the kosher food landscape has exploded with new ideas, I try to stay true to my Hungarian heritage and celebrate what we've passed down and preserved for generations. These recipes are worth keeping because they contain heart, beauty, balance, and explosive taste. I like to simplify Hungarian cuisine, so busy working mothers and homemakers alike can enjoy it.

Fluffy challahs with a crusty shell, a bowl of chicken soup with *kneidlach* (matzah balls) and some *lokshen* (thin noodles) floating inside—that's the type of food you'll find on our Shabbos table. Our Shabbos menu stays basically the same from week to week. I'll switch around the type of fish, the recipe for chicken or meat; I'll add seasonal fruits to the compote, or add on a dessert. But overall it's pretty predictable. Shabbos is when we like to stay true to our Chassidishe heritage and enjoy the *heimish* and oh-so-good Shabbos *macholim* (food) that's been passed down and preserved for generations. It's more than their flavors; it's mostly about their spirit. These dishes represent tradition, each one full of meaning, symbolic of our culture, our faith and our commitment. Each dish is sacred, for it represents our beliefs.

לכבוד שבת קודש

Traditional Shabbos Menu

FRIDAY NIGHT MEAL

Fluffy Heimishe Water Challah

Salmon and Gefilte Fish

Chicken Soup

with noodles and/or kneidlech

Chicken/Meat

Ferfel, Potato Kugel

Zeese Mayeren (sweet carrots)

Apple Compote

SHABBOS MORNING MEAL

Fluffy Heimishe Water Challah

Salmon and Gefilte Fish

Cooked Eggs with Onion, Broiled Chicken Liver and *Galle*

(also known as *Gallereta* and/or *P'tcha*)

Chulent

Dessert

לכבוד שבת קודש

Potless Shabbos Cooking

Your Full Shabbos Cooked in the Oven

I know it sounds too good to be true.

It didn't start out that way. At first I baked just gefilte fish and ferfel in the oven, and felt like a brilliant hacker.

But I have a problem. It's called the all-or-nothing personality, which defines a very stubborn nature to do everything in a grandiose manner. There are many big issues that come along with this type of personality, which is why I'm definitely not bragging about it here.

Don't know what I mean? Let me try to explain with an example.

Four years ago, when it came to moving from Boro Park to Lakewood and buying a house, I wanted a mansion. I mean, if I'm moving all the way to Lakewood, it has to be worth it. I told my husband it was either a ten-room house with two acres of land around it, or I'm not moving out of Boro Park.

But since I am working on myself, I came to my senses and we bought a much smaller house, which is still triple the size (at least) of my Boro Park apartment. Plus, the mortgage is much less than my rent in Brooklyn.

Was I the one who thought a tiny, porch-less, two-bedroom apartment with a windowless kitchen and a two-seater kitchen table was better than a small two-story house of my own?

It's comical when I look back. But yes, that was me.

When I discovered that it was possible to use a shortcut and bake the Shabbos food in the oven, that part of me emerged again. Why just gefilte fish? How cool would it be to just pop the entire Shabbos into your oven!

When I talked about it with my friends, they weren't very excited about my wild idea.

"You can skip the soup," they said.

"Listen," I said, "I am testing it! Let's wait and see."

My mother also wasn't very supportive. "Soup needs to bubble on a stove."

But I firmly decided it was worth trying, even just to be able to mentally cross it off my list.

All stubbornness aside, when it actually came down to it, I popped the soup into the oven late Thursday evening, filled with self-doubt. What if it doesn't work?

I was too petrified to peek. I tried to stay busy so I didn't keep berating myself for my foolishness.

Three hours later, I removed two bubbling pans from the oven: the chulent and the soup.

I couldn't resist, and I sat down with my husband for a bowl of chulent right then and there.

"It's really good, no?" (Any recipe developer can relate to this part.)

My husband claimed the chulent was even better than usual.

Friday night, with each spoonful of soup, the smile on my face just kept on getting wider. It was a wonderful feeling.

Before I continue, I must note that success stories like these feed people who suffer from my all-or-nothing personality. It fills them with adrenaline and drives them to insist on following their extravagant dreams. Not a good thing.

How to Cook Your Full Shabbos in the Oven

Note: I cooked all of these dishes at 350° F; they can bake simultaneously in the oven. Just put the soup and chulent in first at 400° F. Then, when you lower the oven to 350° F, you can put in the rest of the food.

To keep warm on Shabbos, I use a hot plate. To prevent the chulent and ferfel from burning, I use an aluminum disposable muffin pan. A muffin pan is more effective than a regular pan because it distributes the heat more evenly. I place the muffin pan overturned on the hot plate and the disposable pan with the food on top of it. Another alternative is keeping your oven on Shabbos mode.

GEFILTE FISH

For Heimishe Gefilte Fish: Place your roll of frozen gefilte fish into a deep 5" x 7" pan (also called a 5-pound oblong pan). Cover with water as you would in a pot. Then season the water as you usually do. I use lots of sugar, a pinch of salt, onion powder, garlic powder and black pepper. Cover the pan tightly and pop into a pre-heated oven at 350° F for 2 hours. That's it!

You can also try my Letcho Gefilte Fish recipe (page 108) or do as my friend does: She smears the whole loaf with jam, no water, then bakes it covered at 350° F for 2 hours. This is also good; I ate it at her home a few times. It's not your standard *heimishe* gefilte fish, and the texture is a bit tougher, but it is very tasty.

SALMON

I always bake salmon, at least most of the time. There are too many recipes out there for baked salmon to count. Go find your favorite!

CHICKEN SOUP

Place all the soup ingredients in a deep 9" x 13" pan. Season with salt and cover well with water. Pop into a preheated oven at 400° F degrees. Bake for 1 hour on 400° F, then lower to 350° F and bake another 2 hours.

What I put into my chicken soup:

A mesh bag with chicken bones, chicken wings, skin and necks.

Another mesh bag with parsnip and onion.

I add squash and carrots, and sometimes celery.

Then I add water and kosher salt. That's it!

POTATO KUGEL

Your favorite recipe.

CHICKEN

Any baked chicken.

Here's a super easy one: pour duck sauce over chicken bottoms. You can mix some regular sweet duck sauce with hot and spicy duck sauce for a tasty, sweet and tangy chicken recipe loved by all!

FERFEL

Pour 1 packet of toasted ferfel into a regular 5" x 7" pan. Add about 2 tablespoons of oil. Season to your liking and mix well. Cover with boiling hot water. Cover pan tightly and carefully pop into a preheated oven at 350° F. Bake for approximately 15 minutes.

COMPOTE

With compote, there are so many variations (see page 186 for some ideas). You can do anything you want: apples and pears, sugar, honey, no sweetener—just follow the same directions.

Directions: Place the apples and/or fruit into a deep 9" x 13" pan. Cover with water, cover pan and bake in a preheated oven at 350° F for 2 hours.

EGGS

Preheat oven to 350° F.

Use a muffin tin. Place 1 egg in each of 12 muffin cups.

Bake in preheated oven for 30 minutes. Remove and plunge baked eggs into a large bowl filled with ice water until cooled completely, about 10 minutes.

CHULENT

In a deep 9" x 13" pan, add a bit of oil and sauté your diced onion on the stove. Yes, you can sauté right in the pan—just be careful not to do it on a high flame, as it can burn quickly. Once you sauté your onions you can brown your meat (optional). Then add in the beans and the rest of the spices as you usually do. (See page 88 for my chulent recipe.) Cover with water, plus a bit extra. Cover the pan tightly and bake at 400° F for one hour. Lower the heat to 350° F and bake an additional two hours, or more.

Check periodically to see if you need more water. Add more water to the pan before rewarming for Shabbos so that it does not dry out overnight.

Erev Shabbos
Thursday Night Supper

With so much to do Erev Shabbos, Thursday night dinner can be a hassle—after all, we need to cook for Shabbos and still feed the family. Here are a couple of easy supper ideas you can whip up together with your Shabbos food.

Growing up, my Mom always served us chicken soup meatballs or regular chicken bottoms, which she cooked in the soup especially for Thursday night dinner. For sides, there were always one or two salads: a savory salad, such as potato salad, and a sweet salad, like carrot salad or Waldorf salad. These salads are convenient options, because they are good refrigerated and can be served the next day. It's great having them around to enjoy again on hectic Fridays for snack or lunch. It's a "tradition" I definitely took on! For these salads, I love using the Pyrex bowls that come with a rubber lid—the bowl looks presentable on its own, and with the convenient lid, the leftovers are easily stored in the fridge for Friday.

Most often, I make potato kugel, a salad or two, and cook up a big pot of traditional *russel* with extra chicken to serve the children (recipe on page 64); I buy a fresh challah, and that's it!

Another lifesaver on Thursdays and long Fridays: cold cuts! I like to buy at least two different types, one turkey and one pastrami/salami/corned beef, and make cold cuts sandwiches. I let the kids choose their favorite condiments (such as ketchup, mustard, or BBQ sauce), smear it on bread or rolls, pile on the cold cuts of their choice, add in pickles or coleslaw, and supper is done!

Many serve things like ferfel (recipe on page 182) on Thursday—they intentionally make a lot more than will actually be eaten on Friday night, so there's enough for Thursday night supper, too.

Personally, when I cook food for Shabbos, I like it to be for Shabbos. I don't like to serve that special Shabbos food before Shabbos—I like when it's tasted first on Shabbos, and it feels so exciting that way.

However, I must mention that there is a very widespread *minhag* we call *To'ameha*: It is considered a great a mitzva to taste the Shabbos food every Friday afternoon, to ensure that it is tasty and fit to be served at the holy Shabbos meal.

Chicken Soup Meatballs

Yield: approximately 23 balls, depending on size

I like to take ground chicken, form little balls, and pop them into the hot chicken soup that's already cooking on the stove. It takes about 20 minutes to cook, and you get chicken balls that are super-tasty and succulent from cooking in the chicken soup. Paired with ferfel or any side you've prepared plenty of, dinner is served!

Sometimes, when I want to be "fancy," I like to serve these chicken soup meatballs in a bowl of soup along with spiralized veggies (like squash, beets, and carrots), which I buy readymade at my local supermarket.

Ingredients

1 pound ground chicken

1 egg

½ cup plain breadcrumbs (optional)

¾ teaspoon salt

¼ teaspoon black pepper

Directions

Combine all the ingredients and mix to incorporate. Form the mixture into balls. Cook in the chicken soup for 15 to 20 minutes.

Note: I personally don't add any additional spices to the meatball mixture, because I don't want it to affect the pure taste of our traditional chicken soup, but feel free to add your favorite seasoning.

Russel ראסל

Yield: 10–12 servings

Russel is a dish made out of onions, garlic, and chicken wings, traditionally served on Thursday night or Friday for *To'ameha.*

A great russel is all about getting a good, concentrated *zaft* (sauce), which is then enjoyed with challah.

The base starts off similar to the Hungarian chicken paprikash, with lots of onions and paprika, and also simmers on a low flame for 6 to 12 hours.

I use my Instant Pot for this recipe, and using the pressure cooker feature, I have a delicious russel in less than an hour.

In an Instant Pot: Use the Sauté option until the water is added. Then switch to the Meat/Stew feature and cook for about 45 minutes.

Ingredients

1 cup canola oil

2 large Spanish onions, diced

7 cloves garlic, crushed

⅓ cup paprika

2 pounds chicken wings

2 tablespoons onion powder

3 tablespoons kosher salt

¾ teaspoon freshly ground black pepper

Water

Directions

Heat the oil in a large 8-quart pot. Add the onions and sauté them low and slow for a good 15 minutes, until translucent.

Add the garlic and paprika, stirring constantly for about 2 minutes. Add the chicken wings and mix everything together well, sautéing for 3 to 5 minutes, until the wings appear golden.

Add in the rest of the seasonings and mix well. Add approximately 6 cups water. (You want the water to cover, but not too much water, so that the sauce is still pretty thick and doesn't become too diluted.) Cover the pot and bring to a boil. Once bubbling, reduce the flame to low and cook for a minimum of 4 hours (up to 12 hours).

Note: Very often, I'll add a whole chicken breast (with the skin and bones) to cook with the russel, which I then serve to the children for Thursday night dinner or on Shabbos. Although russel traditionally is made with only wings, the chicken breast comes out delicious in there! It's super tasty, and not at all dry; it's moist and shreds easily, the way I love...

Thursday Dinner Salads

Potato Salad

Yield: approximately 6 servings

Ingredients

6 potatoes, whole and unpeeled

5–6 hardboiled eggs, sliced

approximately 6 Israeli pickles, diced

1½ cups sweet corn

½ cup mayonnaise

¼ teaspoon salt

Dash of freshly ground black pepper

Directions

Place the potatoes in a pot and fill with water to cover the potatoes. Cover and cook over medium heat for about 45 minutes, until the potatoes are tender.

Remove from heat, drain, and allow the potatoes to cool a bit.

Once the potatoes are cool enough to handle, remove the peels and cube.

In a bowl, combine the potatoes and the rest of the ingredients.

Serve at room temperature.

Carrot Salad

Yield: 6–8 servings

Ingredients

6 thick loose carrots, shredded

3 yellow apples, shredded

1 (15-ounce) can crushed pineapple

2 cups orange juice

Directions

Toss the ingredients together and refrigerate until ready to serve.

Waldorf Salad

Yield: approximately 4 servings

Ingredients

2 Red Delicious apples, unpeeled and diced

2 Granny Smith apples, unpeeled and diced

3 stalks celery, peeled and finely chopped

1 (20-ounce) can pineapple tidbits, with juice

2 tablespoons mayonnaise

Directions

Combine the apples, celery, and canned pineapple tidbits in a bowl.

Add the mayonnaise to the pineapple juice and mix everything together well.

Serve cold or at room temperature.

Shabbos Staples

Few things evoke such warm sentiments as baking challah … It's a mitzvah and a labor of love—a process that gives back, in the most therapeutic way…

I think many of us end up using our mother's challah recipe, and when it comes to challah, everyone appreciates something else—some people like their challah heavy, some like it sweet. Personally, I'm all about the fluffy, light-as-air water challahs.

This is my mother's challah recipe, which she spent a lot of time testing through trial and error until it was perfect. And although my challahs are definitely fluffy and delicious, they're still not like my mother's. Not just because my mother's challahs are bigger, but because challah is one of those things that becomes personal. I believe the very same recipe will taste different and individual, when different people prepare it.

If you appreciate fluffy, airy challah, I'll tell you this: when it comes to fluffy challah, it's not just about the recipe. Yes, of course you need a great recipe and quality ingredients, but a lot of it is about the process as well.

One of my biggest tips for achieving the ultimate fluffy challah is letting your challah dough rise until it doubles in size at *every* step and stage of the process.

So I make a big deal out of baking challah, because my challah process is sort of a big deal. I remember once trying a quick challah recipe, and finally understanding how easy making challah can be … but I want the kind of results I get from my process, so to me, the whole thing is worth it.

My second tip is that your mood matters.

I've always said this about the challah-making process: it senses my mood. Through experience, I've learned that to get the fluffy results I want, I must be super-patient and not be on the clock. If I'm itching to get the process done, or to get out of the house, my challah dough feels it. Even my husband knows this by now; he's seen it with his own eyes. When the dough is "klutzy," or when the challah comes out of the oven and I'm not so happy because it's a bit heavier than I like, I'll usually admit it's because I did it *"chap-lop"*—really fast or under pressure. Because making fluffy challah is all about letting it rise again and again, and the amount of time the dough needs to rise will vary depending on the weather and room temperature, there's no definite amount of time the process will take.

CHOOSING A CHALLAH BRAID

There are so many beautiful *minhagim* when it comes to the way we braid (or don't braid) our challah.

There's a popular *minhag* to braid challah with six strands, so that the two loaves together, as *Lechem Mishneh*, represent the 12 loaves of the *Lechem Hapanim* that were baked in the *Beis Hamikdosh* every Erev Shabbos.

Many Chassidim make a straight, unbraided challah for the Friday night meal, and a braided challah for the meal on Shabbos day. There are several reasons for this. One beautiful explanation is that, just as the *Zohar* says, the three meals of Shabbos are an allusion to our three Avos: Avraham, Yitzchak and Yaakov. During the Yom Tov of Sukkos, every day a different member of the *Ushpizin* comes to visit. Yet the *Zohar* says that Avraham Avinu comes along each day. The same is true of the three meals of Shabbos: the first meal alludes to Avraham Avinu, when only Avraham comes himself—that's why there's a straight challah. But at the other two meals, which allude to Yitzchok and Yaakov, Avraham Avinu comes along too—therefore, we use a braided challah to hint that Avraham Avinu is present as well.

Practically speaking: when it comes to braiding smaller challahs (anything less than a large challah), I find the fewer strands there are, the fluffier the challah will be. Therefore, I just braid my medium with three strands, and use four strands for large challahs. I love braiding with six or eight strands—I even find it therapeutic—yet I find it takes away from the fluffiness.

Lately, I've been making lots of the football-shaped challah, and I love it. Why? First, it's our *minhag* for Friday night challah. But I also like it for practical reasons: less braiding and less playing around with those precious air bubbles in the dough = even fluffier challah. And if I'm low on energy, I use this method as a way of saving time.

ADDITIONAL TIPS:

- I'm very particular about the brands I use for my challah ingredients—all brands of flour and yeast are not alike.

- Since the salt isn't added together with the other ingredients, it's easy to forget it. I always put the container of salt on the counter at the beginning, when I'm adding the rest of the ingredients. This way, I know I'll see the container afterward (after the challah has kneaded a bit and I've done a few other things in that time…) and it'll remind me.

- When it comes to braiding challah, braid it very loosely, to provide room for growth. When you braid your challah tightly, it looks pretty at the time, but the strands often tear as the challah rises in the oven.

- For the ultimate shiny brown crust, give the challah a second good coating with the egg wash. I find it really makes a difference.

- When freezing the challah, I bake the challah for only 50 minutes, all in the pan. Then I remove the challah from the pans and freeze them in Ziploc bags. When I remove the challah from the freezer, I let them fully defrost, then I bake them in a preheated 400° F oven for the additional 10 minutes (no pan needed). This results in challah that tastes fresh with a super crispy crust.

Mommy's Fluffy Challah

Yield: 6–8 medium challahs

Ingredients

Dough

6 pounds Quality High-Gluten Flour

¼ cup oil

4 eggs

4 tablespoons Fleischmann's Instant Dry Yeast

½–¾ cup sugar

6 cups warm water

3 tablespoons kosher salt

Toppings

2–3 eggs, beaten

Sesame seeds

Poppy seeds

Directions

Place three-quarters of the bag of flour in the metal bowl of your mixer. Dig 2 holes in the flour, and place the oil and eggs in one, and yeast and sugar in the other.

Add the 6 cups warm water and mix on low speed for about 3 minutes until well incorporated. When the dough is formed, add the rest of the flour and salt.

Using the mixer, knead the dough on low for at least 10 minutes. Then cover the bowl with a towel and allow the dough to rise, until it reaches the top of the mixer bowl.

Once the challah dough has doubled in size, press down the dough and mix on low for a bit. Then transfer the dough to another, larger bowl. Sprinkle the dough with some flour, cover with a towel, and allow to rise for about an hour or until it doubles in size.

Recite the *bracha* and remove a piece of dough.

Divide the dough into sections for your preferred braid or shape. Knead each section by hand 2 to 4 times. Cover the sections with a towel and allow to rise again until doubled in size.

Meanwhile, prepare your pans by lining them with parchment paper.

Once the dough has doubled in size, keep the majority of the dough covered while you work on one challah at a time. Braid your challahs and place in the lined pans.

Once done braiding all the challahs, allow them to rise one last time in their pans until they double in size again, about 20 minutes.

Preheat oven to 400° F.

Smear each challah with egg wash and sprinkle with the toppings of your choice.

Bake at 400° F for 20 to 25 minutes (so it develops that nice color).

Reduce oven temperature to 350° F, and bake for an additional 30 minutes.

Remove the challahs from the pans and return them to the oven to bake without the pan for another 10 minutes.

Note: Each oven's baking time will be different. Through trial and error, you'll figure out what works best for your oven.

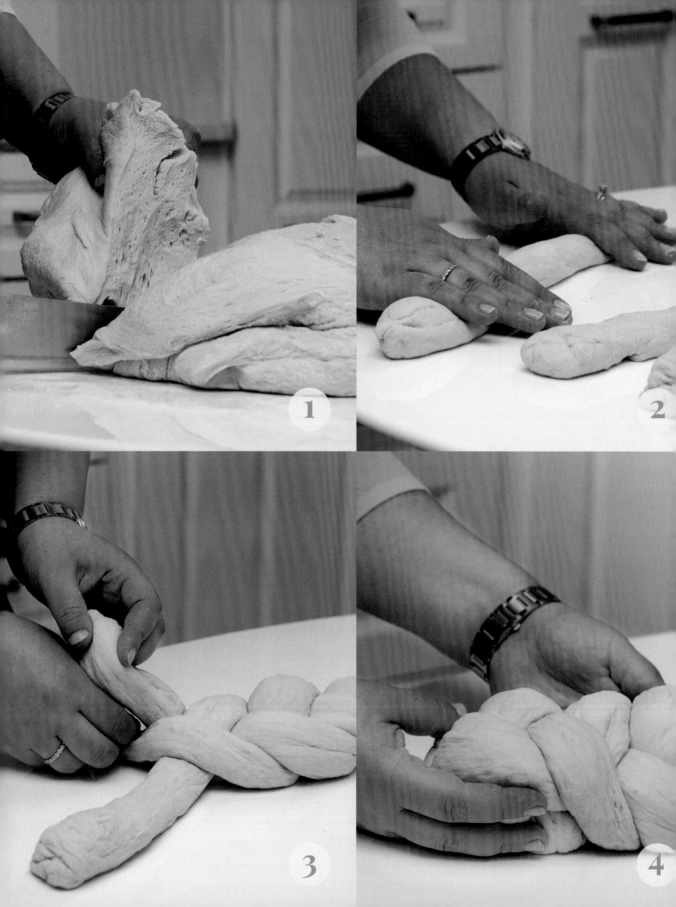

How To Make a Football-Shaped Challah:

Sometimes I make my football-shaped challah with a simple strand in the center. Other times, when I'm feeling fancy, I twist two strands together to form a pretty rope and then place that in the center of my loaf.

To form the challah, simply cut a small piece of dough off to use for the middle rope part. Tuck the main portion of dough into the pan. Roll the small piece of dough into a long strand, and then place it in the center, tucking the ends of the strands beneath the challah.

Chicken Soup

Yield: 10–12 quarts

For the ultimate *kreftig*, hearty soup, I like to use a combination of chicken wings, chicken bones with skin, and some turkey necks, along with vegetables. This, however, is not set in stone—sometimes I'll use chicken legs in place of the turkey necks, and sometimes I cook the chicken soup with celery, which adds a great taste. I also sometimes add knob celery root or fresh parsley for taste, when I feel like it.

This recipe is for a 16-quart pot, because when I make chicken soup, I like to have extra to freeze. I use the frozen chicken soup on hectic weeks when I appreciate being able to take something extra off my list. I also use containers of frozen chicken soup for added flavor in many recipes and soups that call for chicken broth or chicken stock. Feel free to halve this recipe for an 8-quart pot.

Ingredients

3–4 pounds chicken bones

1 pound chicken wings

2–3 turkey necks

2 parsnips, peeled

1 Spanish onion

5 thick carrots, peeled

2 zucchini, unpeeled

4–5 tablespoons kosher salt

Optional Add-Ins

Celery

Parsley

Directions

Start off by organizing all the flavor components in mesh cooking bags.

Bag #1: Chicken bones, chicken wings, skin and turkey necks.

Bag #2: Parsnips and onion.

Begin loading the 16-quart pot, putting in the vegetables you'll use, like the carrots and squash, first. Then place the bags of bones, which will be discarded or set aside after the soup is done cooking, on top.

Add the salt and fill the pot with water.

Bring to a boil over a high flame until bubbling. Then reduce heat to medium-low and cook for 30 minutes. Then reduce heat again to low and cook for another 3 hours.

Tip: I like to put all the chicken wings, bones, skin, and necks in a mesh cooking bag—this way it's easier to remove them, and it also keeps the soup clean and clear, as most of the residue stays in the bag. You can find these mesh bags in most supermarkets, usually next to the produce section.

Traditional Fluffy Matzah Balls
Kneidlech • קניידלעך

Yield: 15–18, depending on size

Ingredients

4 large eggs

4 tablespoons vegetable oil

½ cup water or seltzer

1 cup matzah meal

1 teaspoon salt

Directions

In a bowl, mix the eggs, oil, and water. Add in the matzah meal and salt and mix well.

Refrigerate for about an hour to set.

Form the mixture into small balls. Add the balls to your cooking chicken soup or a pot of boiling water with a bit of salt.

Cook the matzah balls for 30 minutes, covered.

Leave the matzah balls in the soup if serving soon, or transfer to a container and refrigerate until ready to use.

Tip: Use oiled hands to shape the kneidlech into smooth, perfectly round balls.

Big-Batch Cream of Chicken Soup recipe on next page.

Big-Batch Cream of Chicken Soup

I've been making cream of chicken soup for years, and for good reason. I come from an ultra-traditional background, and my grandmother serves only pure chicken soup at every Yom Tov. At every meal.

I serve traditional chicken soup every Shabbos, but when it comes to Yom Tov, I like changing it up.

Cream of chicken soup was my first venture outside … It didn't feel that unfamiliar, and it's comforting and appealing to everyone. Every time.

I know that many add potatoes to thicken the consistency of the soup even more, but I find it unnecessary, and with all the challah, I think we've got more than enough carbs!

Chicken cubes alone add just a mild flavor to the broth, which is why I also add in chicken wings, chicken bones, and turkey necks. I don't want it tasting like a zucchini soup. This cream of chicken soup is, as we say in Yiddish, *kreftig,* with a real depth of flavor.

Ingredients

4–5 mesh cooking bags

5 pounds chicken wings

2½ pounds chicken bones

1.3 pounds turkey necks

5 pounds chicken tenders, cubed

10 large zucchini, peeled

6 cloves fresh garlic

4 tablespoons kosher salt

1 teaspoon ground black pepper

17 cups water

Directions

Place the chicken bones, chicken wings, and turkey necks in mesh cooking bags.

Using a good pair of kitchen shears, cut the raw chicken tenders into bite-sized pieces and place the pieces into a mesh bag or two.

Tip: An easy way to fill the bags is to spread the edges of the bag over a bowl. This way, the mesh bag remains open, and you can easily toss in the pieces as you cut them.

Place the mesh bags into an 18-quart pot. Place the peeled zucchini into the pot.

Add fresh garlic, salt, and pepper.

Add water to just about cover the other ingredients.

Cover the pot and bring the soup to a boil. Then reduce the heat to medium and cook for a good 4 hours.

Once done, remove the mesh bags with the bones, wings, and necks and discard.

Remove and set aside the mesh bags of cubed chicken.

Using an immersion blender, blend the zucchini well until fully incorporated.

Cut open the mesh bags and pour the cubed chicken into the pot of soup.

Notes:

• Using mesh cooking bags makes the process a breeze! No need to fish around for pieces of zucchini or chicken after it's done cooking.

• This recipe is a big one—it uses an 18-quart pot, because that's just the way I roll. Sometimes. I cook up a big pot before every Yom Tov season because this soup is our favorite and freezes well. Feel free to halve the recipe.

Chulent

Yield: approximately 8 servings

I'll admit: Although I never follow a recipe, I'm a very good intuitive cook and I make a great-tasting chulent by pouring in a little bit of this and a lot of that … *baruch Hashem!* But here's the "big admit" part: not too long ago, my chulent burned or dried out every second week … and although it tasted great, it was a disaster. At one point, I got so tired of all the flops, I went on a chulent-cooking strike … At the time, I cooked my chulent in a pot. Why I never got a Crock-Pot is beyond me! I have every machine you can imagine in my kitchen, including an Instant Pot, a Bosch mixer, a Kitchen-Aid mixer, a Vitamix blender, a Breville juicer, a sandwich maker, a panini maker, a waffle maker, a Betty Crocker pizza maker—and the list goes on. Why I only got a Crock-Pot after almost 10 years of marriage is one of those things I'll never understand … maybe it's because my mother cooks delicious chulent in a pot? Or because for years, I was successful doing that too? Until I wasn't…

Anyway, I got a nice Crock-Pot, and that was the end of the struggle! Now we have the most delicious chulent with the perfect consistency every week. If you don't have a Crock-Pot yet, I suggest that you don't wait 10 years. Get yourself a Deluxe Slow Cooker *lekoved Shabbos Kodesh*. I have one made by Magic Mill which is really nice because it's made out of steel, rather than earthenware, which means I can put it on my stovetop either to sauté the onions or re-warm the food in a jiffy. It's also got a great nonstick base, comfortable handles, and a flat reversible glass cover, which allows you to turn the cover over and place additional food on top to warm.

Chulent is not just chulent at our house—we literally roll out a whole chulent buffet. Beyond the basic meat and beans, I add jachnun, kishka, kielbasa (see the add-ins below for ideas), changing it up every week.

Tip: Instead of adding water, I like to use chicken soup—it adds so much depth of flavor! Sometimes I add pieces of chicken to the chulent as well; it comes out really tasty in there!

Ingredients

1 tablespoon canola oil

1 onion, diced

1 pound meat (usually chulent meat, which is generally second-cut brisket or shank kolichel)

1 (16-ounce) bag great northern beans, soaked in water

chicken soup or water, to cover

2 cloves fresh garlic, crushed

3½ tablespoons paprika

1 tablespoon onion soup mix

1½ teaspoons salt

½ teaspoon black pepper

¼ cup ketchup

½ cup barley

peeled potatoes, quartered (optional)

Add-Ins

Frozen jachnun

Kishka

Eggs

Marrow bones

Navel pastrami

Kielbasa

Directions

Heat the oil in an 8-quart Crock-Pot on high heat. Add the diced onions and sauté until soft and golden.

Once the onions are sautéed, add the meat and beans and cover with the liquid. Add the garlic, spices, and ketchup and mix well with the beans and meat. If you're adding in pieces of potatoes, add them now.

Add the barley on top, plus any additional add-ins you would like to add, such as kishka, jachnun or marrow bones. Add water if needed, to make sure everything is covered in water. Cook on high for about 5 hours.

Before Shabbos, make sure there's enough water covering the chulent and then set the Crock-Pot to low.

Note: Slow cookers each behave somewhat differently—it may be necessary to adjust cooking times and heat levels to work for your model.

Kishka • מעהל קוגל

Yield: 4 slices

I love this sweet kishka recipe from one of my favorite personal chefs, Gitty Frankel. I actually never liked kishka until I tried this one, when Gitty sent me supper as a *kimpeturin*. If you've never made your own kishka, I urge you to try … it's really not as hard as you might think, and commercial-tasting store-bought kishka simply can't compare.

I cook this recipe in my chulent, but I also use it in other ways, such as stuffing chicken capons.

Ingredients

1 cup + 2 tablespoons all-purpose flour

¼ cup sugar

1 tablespoon paprika

½ teaspoon salt

½ cup hot water

Approximately ⅓ cup oil

Directions

Place the flour, sugar, and spices in a large bowl. Add the hot water and oil and mix very well.

Prepare a piece of parchment paper. Place the kishka mixture in the center of the parchment paper, then roll up the parchment paper to form a loaf shape. Cinch the open ends well, twisting tightly closed.

Tip: Wet the parchment paper, then wring out and flatten the paper before using it to wrap the kishka filling—the damp paper will be easier to roll, shape, and cinch.

Fish

Tzadikim throughout the generations have placed great importance on eating fish *lekoved Shabbos*. The Baal Shem Tov received a choice from Heaven of where he would like to live, in the city of Nemrov, or in Mezbish. He chose Mezbish, because there it was easier to get fish *lekoved Shabbos*.

(זכרון טוב)

Heimishe Salmon with Kotchenyu

Yield: 4 servings

This is your typical salmon, sweet and tasty. By adding sufficient pike skin, you'll *b'ezras Hashem* get a nice kotchenyu (gelled sauce) with it!

Tip: These days, many fish brands make a "fish gelling" powder, which is sold in a typical spice container. Although I usually use pike skin, I like to have gelling powder on hand, for when I don't have pike skin and want to make a kotchenyu. I have found that the powder always works.

Note: The recipe is for salmon, but you can cook your gefilte fish along with it as well. If you want to cook the gefilte in the same pot, cook the gefilte first for an hour, then add the salmon.

Ingredients

4 (6-ounce) slices salmon

1 large onion, sliced

4 (2-ounce) packages pike
   skin, in mesh cooking bags

6 cups water

1½ cups sugar

2 tablespoons paprika

1 teaspoon salt

1 teaspoon black pepper

Directions

In a 6-quart pot over high heat, boil the water with the onion and pike skin. Once bubbling, add the spices and stir well. Add the salmon to the boiling water and cook for 15 minutes over medium-high heat, at a constant boil.

Remove from heat and allow to cool completely before removing the slices from the pot, to avoid breaking.

Transfer the fish to a glass or Pyrex dish with a cover (or a container) and refrigerate.

Serve cold.

Tip: I transfer the slices of fish along with a bit of sauce, and then pour additional sauce into a plastic or Pyrex container, close tightly, and refrigerate, so I have additional kotchenyu separately. The sauce will take on a jelled consistency as it is refrigerated overnight.

Heimeishe Gefilte

Yield: 1 roll gefilte fish

Your typical *heimishe* sweet gefilte fish. Always a winner!

Ingredients

1 roll gefilte fish

¾ cup sugar

2 tablespoons salt

1 tablespoon onion powder

1 teaspoon garlic powder

1 teaspoon black pepper

Directions

Add the frozen roll of gefilte fish to large pot and cover with water. Add the sugar and all the spices, and bring to a boil. Once bubbling, reduce heat to low and cook for 2 hours.

Sweet Salmon

Yield: 6–8 portions

Although I most often bake salmon, when I do cook salmon, this is one of my favorite recipes—it's so *heimish*, simple, and sweet.

Ingredients

6–8 (6-ounce) slices salmon

2–3 large Spanish onions, thinly sliced

2 cups sugar

½ cup lemon juice

1 teaspoon salt

2 cups water

Directions

Place a 6- or 8-quart pot over high heat so that it gets nice and hot. Pour the sugar and onions into the pot, then reduce the flame to medium heat. Using a wooden spoon, keep stirring the sugar and onions for 10 to 15 minutes, until the sugar melts into a liquid and the onions get very soft.

Add the salmon to the pot, then add the rest of the ingredients.

Cover the pot and cook for 35 to 40 minutes.

Remove from heat and allow to cool.

Note: Wait until the salmon is completely cooled before transferring the salmon from the pot to your pan or container. Warm salmon is more likely to fall apart.

Letcho Salmon

Yield: sauce for up to 18 servings

Coming from a super-traditional home, I never would have dreamed that one day, I would be serving Letcho (Lescó, in Hungarian) at a Shabbos meal. Growing up, Shabbos food was purely *Shabbos'dig* and was not served during the week, unless it was leftovers. The food served at the Shabbos meal wasn't just classified by type, but by how it was cooked … pepper letcho was *vuchen'dig* (weekday), and while it was a better weekday meal, it still wasn't a traditional Shabbos kind of fish.

When I got married, I discovered that my *Shvigger* (mother-in-law), a *balabuste* in her own right, served letcho salmon every week, and that's how it became my new tradition!

This is our all-time favorite Shabbos fish recipe. Since I keep making it (I serve this fish almost every week), I have plenty of tips!

• Since the letcho (pepper sauce) recipe yields a large quantity, I divide the sauce according to the amount I use each Shabbos, and freeze it in containers. On Thursday or Erev Shabbos, I defrost a container of letcho, pour it over the fresh salmon in the pan, cover the pan, and pop it into the oven. Bam! Gourmet Shabbos fish, all ready.

• I serve this fish warm (it's only good warm, in my opinion), so I keep it on a hot plate.

Kick it up: If you like a little heat in your food, add some cubed hot peppers or harissa to the letcho. Yum.

Health tip: If you're on a special diet, you can swap in: **Coconut aminos** *instead of soy sauce,* **onion powder** *instead of onion soup mix,* **tomato sauce** *instead of ketchup.*

Ingredients

**Salmon fillet slices
(up to 18 slices)**

Letcho Sauce:

2 onions, diced

¼ cup oil, for sautéing

2 red bell peppers, diced

2 orange bell peppers, diced

2 yellow bell peppers, diced

2 green bell peppers, diced

4 beef tomatoes, diced

**1–2 hot peppers (fresh or jarred), diced
(for heat—optional)**

2 cloves garlic, crushed (fresh or frozen)

¼ cup soy sauce

½ cup ketchup

1 tablespoon onion soup mix

1 teaspoon salt

½ teaspoon black pepper

Directions

Sauté the onions in oil, until soft. Add the peppers and sauté on high for approximately 20 minutes, giving it a good stir every few minutes. Add the tomatoes and sauté for another 5 minutes. Add the remaining ingredients and seasonings. Cover and cook for 45 minutes on low.

Preheat oven to 350° F. Place the salmon fillet slices in a pan. Pour the letcho sauce over the salmon and cover the pan. Bake at 350° F for 1 hour. Serve warm.

Garlic Dill Salmon

Yield: 2 servings

This is one of my go-to recipes, for when I'm short on prep time and want something fine.

It's full of herbs and pungent lemon and garlic flavor.

Ingredients

2 (6-ounce) slices salmon fillet

Sauce

6 tablespoons lemon juice

2 teaspoons chopped fresh dill

4 cloves garlic, crushed

4 tablespoons extra virgin olive oil

¼ teaspoon salt

Dash of freshly ground black pepper

Directions

Combine the sauce ingredients and mix well.

Place the salmon slices in the pan, pour the sauce over the salmon, and cover with foil. Place in the refrigerator to marinate for a couple of hours.

Preheat oven to 375° F.

Bake at 375° F for 15 minutes, covered. Uncover the pan and bake for an additional 12 minutes.

Note: When baking salmon, I love to use Scottish salmon—it's a bit more pricey, but totally worth it.

Honey Mustard Salmon

Yield: 4 servings

This is not your typical honey mustard salmon! Sweet and tasty, the balance of flavors in this dish is just perfect.

Ingredients

4 (6-ounce) slices salmon fillet, skinned

2 tablespoons spicy brown mustard

1 tablespoon honey

2 teaspoons chopped fresh dill

½ cup honey-glazed pecans, coarsely chopped

Lemon wedges (optional)

Directions

Preheat oven to 400° F. Line a baking sheet with parchment paper or coat with non-stick cooking spray.

Place the salmon slices on the prepared baking sheet.

In a small bowl, whisk together the mustard, honey, and dill.

Generously spread the mustard mixture on top of all the salmon slices. Evenly sprinkle the pecans on top of the slices.

Bake at 400° F for 15 minutes, until the salmon flakes easily.

Serve with lemon wedges, if preferred.

Succulent Orange Salmon

Yield: 4 servings

This orange salmon is sweet, unique and so moist!

Ingredients

2 (6-ounce) slices salmon fillet

½ navel orange, sliced

Sauce

2 tablespoons soy sauce

2 tablespoons brown sugar

2 cloves garlic, minced

¼ cup orange juice

1 tablespoon maple syrup

Directions

Combine all the sauce ingredients in a large bowl.

Place the salmon fillets flesh-side down in the bowl with the marinade. Place in the refrigerator to marinate for at least 10 minutes.

Preheat oven to 375° F.

Place the salmon fillets skin-side down in a Pyrex baking dish. Top with slices of orange and bake at 375° F for 15 minutes.

Letcho Gefilte

Yield: 1 roll gefilte fish

Ever tried gefilte fish warm, cooked in a delectable savory sauce?

Letcho gefilte is a beautiful, tasty appetizer to serve *lekoved Shabbos* or Yom Tov. Especially when there are a few days of Yom Tov, and salmon can get boring, I find this gefilte fish version handy, as it's a great *"mechubadige"* way to serve gefilte fish. It's similar to my letcho salmon recipe, though not the same.

Ingredients

1 roll plain gefilte fish

4 tablespoons canola oil

2 onions, diced

2 cloves garlic, crushed (fresh or frozen)

1 beefsteak tomato, diced

1 red pepper, diced

1 teaspoon salt

½ teaspoon freshly ground black pepper

1 teaspoon onion powder

½ cup ketchup

Directions

Preheat oven to 350° F.

Heat the oil in a 3-quart pot. Add the diced onions and sauté over medium-high heat for about 5 minutes, until onions are softened. Add the garlic, diced tomato, and diced pepper and keep stirring for another 2 to 5 minutes.

Season with salt, pepper, onion powder and ketchup and mix until everything is well incorporated. Cover the pot and cook for another 5 to 10 minutes over medium heat.

Remove the wrapper from the frozen gefilte fish roll and place the roll in a deep 5" x 7" pan. Pour the letcho mixture over the gefilte fish and cover the pan well.

Bake at 350° F for 2 hours.

Remove from oven, slice, and serve warm.

Salmon Salad with Creamy Shallot Dressing

Yield: 4 servings

This salmon is delicious on its own, served as a whole slice, but it's even better served over a bed of fresh veggies along with this creamy shallot dressing. I adore this dressing—it's not your typical 1-2-3 mixed mayo and spices dressing, and that's exactly what I love about it! Shallots are one of my favorite members of the onion family; they are sweeter than the typical white or red onion, and add a really nice flavor when sautéed or grilled.

The dressing totally elevates this salad to restaurant-worthy, gourmet fare, perfect for *Shalosh Seudos*, a Yom Tov meal, or anytime!

Ingredients

Salmon

4 (6-ounce) slices salmon fillet, cut into cubes

2 tablespoons brown sugar

1 teaspoon paprika

1 teaspoon chili powder

1 teaspoon kosher salt

½ teaspoon garlic powder

⅛ teaspoon cayenne pepper (optional)

2 tablespoons lime juice

1 tablespoon olive oil

Dressing

Oil, for sautéing

5 shallots, cut into rings

4 tablespoons vegetable oil

2 tablespoons lemon juice

3 tablespoons water

½ teaspoon mustard

1 teaspoon honey

1 teaspoon kosher salt

¼ teaspoon freshly ground black pepper

Salad

16 ounces greens (arugula or romaine lettuce)

1 carrot, julienned

1½ cups cherry tomatoes, halved

Whole shelled pistachios

Directions

Salmon

Preheat oven to 400° F. Line a large, rimmed baking sheet with foil, and lightly brush the foil with oil.

In a shallow bowl, mix together brown sugar, paprika, chili powder, salt, garlic, cayenne pepper, and lime juice together.

Pat the salmon fillets dry and then pat the seasoning mixture onto the top surface of each piece of salmon to coat. Place the salmon on the lined baking sheet.

Bake at 400° F for about 15 minutes.

Dressing

Heat oil in a small frying pan over a high flame. Add the shallots and sauté for about 3 minutes, then reduce heat to medium-low and sauté for another 10 to 15 minutes, until soft and golden. Remove from heat.

In a blender (or food processor), combine the oil, lemon juice, water, mustard, honey, salt, pepper and sautéed shallots, and process until the dressing has a creamy consistency.

Assemble

Place the greens on a plate, top with veggies and salmon, then drizzle with dressing and garnish with pistachios.

Salmon Salad with Creamy Shallot Dressing

Dips & Salads

Homemade dips are so delicious, because they're fresh and pure, without any unnecessary ingredients.

I believe that dips really don't need exact measurements, but since many enjoy the security of a recipe, I measured them out for you. Nonetheless, remember that these recipes are not *"Toras Moshe"* and you can adjust them, adding more mayonnaise or less garlic, etc., according to your taste…

Eggplant Babaganoush

Yield: approximately 1½ (1-lb) containers

Ingredients

1 large eggplant

1¼ cups mayonnaise

2 cloves garlic, crushed

½ teaspoon salt

½ teaspoon black pepper

Directions

Wrap the eggplant well in foil, and place it on the grill or over an open flame on the stovetop. Using tongs, keep turning the eggplant—as one side gets cooked and feels soft, turn it to another side, until the entire eggplant is soft.

Once the eggplant is cooked, allow it to cool a bit, so it's easier to handle.

Unwrap the foil. Remove the inside flesh and seeds of the eggplant and transfer to a bowl. Add the rest of the ingredients to the bowl, and blend using an immersion blender.

Dill Dip

Yield: 1 (1-lb) container

Ingredients

Approximately 6 tablespoons chopped fresh dill

1 clove garlic, crushed

2 cups mayonnaise

Directions

Using a food processor fitted with the S-blade, process the ingredients well.

Tomato Dip

Yield: approximately 1 (1-lb) container

We like our tomato dip to be red and chunky, in the Israeli *"Salat Aravi"* style. If you prefer a smooth orange tomato dip, just let it process a bit longer, and maybe add a bit more oil.

For a spicy tomato dip, add a jarred hot cherry pepper, or red pepper flakes.

Ingredients

2 soft ripe beefsteak tomatoes,
   cut into chunks

2 cloves garlic, crushed

¼ cup oil

½ teaspoon salt

½ teaspoon black pepper

Directions

Using a food processor fitted with the S-blade, blend the ingredients until they reach the desired consistency.

Olive Dip

Yield: 1 (1-lb) container

I like my olive dip to have a bit of texture, so that you can see tiny bits of olives. I use the pimento-stuffed olives, but you can also use plain olives, and if you prefer it with more mayonnaise, you can increase the amount.

Ingredients

1 (7-ounce) jar stuffed olives, drained

1½ cups mayonnaise

Directions

Using an immersion blender or a food processor fitted with the S-blade, blend the olives and mayonnaise together until it reaches the desired consistency.

Roasted Red Pepper Dip

Yield: 1 (1-lb) container

Ingredients

2 red peppers, seeded

1 large juicy beef tomato

1 clove garlic, crushed

½ teaspoon salt

½ teaspoon freshly ground black pepper

¼ teaspoon onion powder

Dash (or two) red pepper flakes

Directions

Preheat oven to 400° F. Line a 9" x 13" baking sheet with foil.

Place the seeded peppers skin-side up on the lined pan.

Roast at 400° F for 25 minutes or until the skin is charred.

Remove from oven and allow to cool.

Remove the skins from the cooled peppers. Place the peeled peppers and the rest of the ingredients in a food processor fitted with the S-blade. Blend until it reaches the desired consistency (I like it chunky).

Tip: You can put the hot roasted peppers into a Ziploc bag and seal it, so that the peppers sweat—then the skins will be easier to remove.

Spicy Chatzilim

Yield: 1–2 (1-lb) containers

This recipe is not Hungarian or European—it's very Israeli and spicy, and that's precisely why some family members love it so much!

Ingredients

1 large eggplant, unpeeled and finely cubed

kosher salt

canola oil

½ cup harissa

3 tablespoons vinegar

2 teaspoons sugar

2–3 tablespoons freshly chopped parsley

Directions

Sprinkle the cubed eggplant with salt, and allow to stand for 30 minutes or more.

Heat ¼ inch of oil in a pan. Fry the eggplant for about 10 minutes, or until soft.

Transfer the fried eggplant to a bowl and toss with the harissa, vinegar, sugar, and parsley.

Refrigerate until ready to serve.

Cucumber Salad

Yield: approximately 4 (1-lb) containers

One of our favorite salads! Always nice as a side, because it's made of fresh vegetables with just the right amount of tanginess.

Ingredients

6 Persian cucumbers, thinly sliced

1 red onion, thinly sliced

1 red pepper, thinly sliced

1 cup lemon juice

½ cup sugar

2 teaspoons fresh dill, chopped

Directions

In a bowl, combine the vegetables with the lemon juice, sugar, and fresh dill.

Transfer to a container, and close the lid tightly. Shake it well and marinate in the refrigerator overnight before serving.

Before serving, shake the container well.

Marinated Pepper Salad

Yield: approximately 2½ (1-lb) containers

This is a simple salad with a short list of fresh ingredients—it tastes great and will look colorful and fantastic among the other delicious food being served. And it'll taste great for up to one week in the fridge.

Ingredients

1 red bell pepper, thinly sliced

1 orange bell pepper, thinly sliced

1 green bell pepper, thinly sliced

1 yellow bell pepper, thinly sliced

1 red onion, thinly sliced

1½ tablespoons salt

4 cups water

½ cup vinegar

½ cup sugar

1–2 tablespoons fresh dill (optional)

Directions

Sprinkle the sliced peppers and onion with salt. Allow to stand at room temperature for at least 30 minutes.

Using a paper towel, squeeze any excess water from the peppers.

In a 3-quart pot over high heat, bring the water, vinegar, and sugar to a boil. Once the mixture is bubbling, stir in the peppers and onions and cook for just 2 minutes. Remove from heat and allow to cool. Stir in the dill.

Transfer to an airtight container with approximately 1 cup of cooking liquid. Marinate in the refrigerator overnight.

Store in the refrigerator for up to 1 week.

Spring Salad with Dill Dressing

Yield: approximately 6 servings

I've noticed that when it comes to naming salads, I always end up putting the seasons in there. And when it comes to fresh, vibrant salads, there will be Spring and Summer involved. However, I don't want you to think these salads are meant to be served only in the Spring and Summer. Oh, no! I think these salads are a *shaliach* to infuse our meals with crisp freshness even in the dead of the winter!

I love this creamy salad dressing, and the pretzel crisps add a great crouton-like crunch to a salad.

Ingredients

8 ounces arugula

½ head romaine lettuce, chopped

8 stalks celery, chopped

6 ounces cherry tomatoes, halved

2 Persian cucumbers, sliced

1 small carrot, julienned

approximately 3 cups pretzel crisps, crushed into pieces

Dill Dressing

1 cup mayonnaise

3 tablespoons vinegar

¼ cup sugar

2 tablespoons water

2 cloves garlic, crushed

¼ cup freshly chopped dill

Directions

Whisk the dressing ingredients in a small bowl (or shake it well in a tightly sealed container).

In a big bowl or on a large platter, spread the arugula and romaine. Top with the rest of the vegetables (as seen in the image, or just distributed randomly).

Drizzle with the dill dressing and top with pieces of pretzel crisps.

Note 1: You will have extra dressing for another time. The dressing keeps well; it can be refrigerated in an airtight container for 2 to 3 months.

Note 2: The cucumbers in the salad were cut with a Borner Wave-Waffle Cutter. They aren't merely pretty—I actually believe they taste better this way!

Summer Salad with Tomato Vinaigrette

Yield: 4–6 servings

I love making this delicious salad, especially in the summer. The grilled onions go so well with the sweet jicama and this incredible tangy tomato vinaigrette. When making it for dinner, I sometimes add grilled steak to the salad.

You don't need an outdoor grill for this—you can grill the onions using a grill pan instead, and if you don't have a grill pan, you can sauté the onions, too!

Ingredients

Salad

2 heads romaine lettuce, leaves torn

1½ pounds assorted heirloom cherry tomatoes, halved

½ jicama, peeled and julienned

Grilled onions

2–3 large red onions, sliced

olive oil

salt

pepper

Vinaigrette

½ cup cherry tomatoes

Juice of 2 limes

2 teaspoons adobo sauce (or sauce from a jar of hot peppers)

1 teaspoon honey

¼ cup extra-virgin olive oil

Kosher salt

Freshly ground pepper

Directions

To prepare the vinaigrette, purée the cherry tomatoes, lime juice, adobo sauce, and honey in a blender or food processor fitted with the S-blade. While the machine is running, add the olive oil and purée until smooth. Season with salt and pepper.

Brush the red onion slices with olive oil, and season with salt and pepper.

Grill the onion, turning occasionally, until softened and charred in spots (about 8 minutes).

To assemble the salad, divide the lettuce among the plates. Top with the grilled onion, heirloom tomatoes, and jicama. Drizzle with the vinaigrette.

Poultry

Chicken Capon Stuffed with Pastrami and Kishka

Yield: 6 servings

The ultimate chicken capon, packed with flavor. I love the combination of sweet homemade kishka and pickled pastrami. The Honey Ginger BBQ Sauce makes this recipe an all-around winner!

Ingredients

6 chicken capons (deboned chicken thighs)

1 (1-pound) navel pastrami

Kishka

1 cup + 2 tablespoons all-purpose flour

¼ cup sugar

1 tablespoon paprika

½ teaspoon salt

⅓–½ cup oil

½ cup hot water

Honey Ginger BBQ Sauce

¼ cup vinegar

¼ cup honey

¼ cup ketchup

1 tablespoon hot sauce

2 large cloves garlic, crushed

1 tablespoon crushed peeled ginger (or 1 cube frozen ginger)

¼ teaspoon salt

Directions

Cook the pastrami. Place the vacuum-packed pastrami in a deep 5" x 7" pan covered with water, and cover the pan.

Bake at 250° F for a minimum of 5 hours. Once done cooking, open the vacuum-sealed bag and remove the pastrami. Pull the pastrami apart using two forks.

Make the Kishka

Place the flour, sugar, and spices in a large bowl. Add the oil and hot water and mix very well.

Prepare the Sauce

In a 2- or 2½-quart heavy saucepan, stir together the sauce ingredients and cook over medium heat uncovered, stirring occasionally, until thickened and reduced (about 8 minutes). Stir frequently toward the end of cooking, to prevent sticking.

Assemble the Capons

Preheat oven to 350° F.

Place the capons skin-side down. Stuff each capon with about 1 tablespoon of kishka filling and 1 tablespoon of cooked navel pastrami. Fold over the two sides of each capon. Place the capons seam-side down in a 9" x 13" pan.

Pour the sauce over the capons and cover the pan.

Bake at 350° F for 1 hour. Uncover and bake for an additional 20 minutes.

Set the oven to broil for an additional 2 to 3 minutes.

Caramelized Chicken and Mushrooms

Yield: 4 servings

An easy recipe that tastes gourmet! I love the earthy flavor of the mushrooms, with the wonderful rich combination of silan, wine, and sautéed onions—tantalizingly perfect for Shabbos.

Ingredients

2 tablespoons oil

1 large onion, cut into rings

8 ounces baby bella mushrooms, quartered

¼ cup silan (or honey)

2 tablespoons red wine

1 clove garlic, crushed

Dash of salt

Dash of black pepper

1 pound (4–6 pieces) chicken cutlets, pounded thin

Directions

Heat the oil in a medium pot over a high flame. Add the onions and sauté for about 4 minutes, until soft. Add the mushrooms, honey, wine, and garlic, and mix to incorporate.

Move the mushroom-and-onion mixture to the side of the pot and add the cutlets to the pot. Baste the cutlets with some of the sauce. Cover the pot and cook for 10 minutes over medium heat. Flip the cutlets onto the other side and cook for another 5 minutes.

Cutlet Roll-Ups in Orange Apricot Sauce

Yield: 10 chicken roll-ups

This recipe takes several steps and pots … But you taste it! Every single pot. It's the real kind of cooking, where you don't take shortcuts and you take the time to sauté the shredded vegetables to maximize their flavor. The results are so divine! These chicken roll-ups, stuffed with mashed potatoes and veggies, taste so delicious and *heimish* and come along with all the warm, homey vibes!

Ingredients

10 chicken cutlets, pounded thin

Filling

3 Yukon Gold potatoes, peeled

1 onion, grated

1 carrot, grated

3 tablespoons vegetable oil

½ teaspoon garlic powder

½ teaspoon salt

dash of freshly ground black pepper

Orange Apricot Sauce

¼ cup orange juice

1 cup apricot jam

¼ cup white wine

paprika, for sprinkling

Directions

Fill a medium pot with water, then add the peeled potatoes and a bit of salt. Make sure the water is covering the potatoes, and bring to a boil. Cook the potatoes over medium-high heat for a couple of minutes, until the potatoes are soft when tested with a fork.

Meanwhile, grate the onion and carrot, either by hand or in a food processor fitted with the "C" fine shredding blade.

Heat the oil in a frypan over a high flame. Add the grated onion and carrot and sauté for a good 8 minutes. Add the salt, pepper, garlic powder and sauté, stirring intermittently, for another 2 to 3 minutes. Remove from heat.

Mash the cooked potatoes and mix with the sautéed vegetables.

Preheat oven to 350° F.

To assemble, open each cutlet flat and place approximately 1 to 2 tablespoons (depending on the size of the cutlet) in the center. Roll the two ends together to close. Place the cutlet seam-side down in a 9" x 13" pan. Repeat with rest of the cutlets.

Whisk the sauce ingredients together in a small bowl, pour the mixture over all the stuffed cutlets, season the chicken with paprika, and cover the pan.

Bake at 350° F for 30 minutes. Uncover and bake for another 10 minutes.

Spicy Apricot Chicken Thighs

Yield: 4 servings

This recipe is one I am very proud of: succulent, spicy, apricot-coated chicken thighs.

If the coating is too spicy for little ones, you can just remove the skin—that's what I do. (And don't worry, the delicious skin doesn't go to waste, "someone" enjoys it a whole lot.)

Ingredients

4 chicken thighs, with skin

¾ cup apricot jam

2 cloves garlic, crushed

½ teaspoon red pepper flakes

¼ teaspoon salt

½ teaspoon black pepper

2 tablespoons white vinegar

Directions

Preheat oven to 350° F.

Combine the sauce ingredients in a bowl and whisk together.

Place the chicken thighs on a baking sheet or 9" x 13" pan. Pour the apricot mixture over the chicken thighs.

Bake uncovered at 350° F for 1 hour.

Remove the pan from the oven and baste the chicken, pouring the surrounding sauce over the thighs.

Return to oven and bake for another 25 minutes.

Chicken Meatloaf with Mushroom Gravy

Yield: approximately 4 servings

All of the classic flavors of meatloaf shine in this recipe, thanks to the Worcestershire sauce, which adds a familiar-tasting depth of flavor that will surprise you.

The rich mushroom gravy makes this meatloaf special, suitable to serve at your Shabbos Table! I skipped the complicated steps and fancy techniques and used my "cheating" method of just adding the flour at the end to thicken the gravy.

Ingredients

Chicken Meatloaf

1½ pounds ground chicken

½ cup bread crumbs

2 eggs

1 tablespoon ketchup

1 teaspoon Worcestershire sauce (fish-free)

½ teaspoon salt

black pepper

Mushroom Gravy

3 tablespoons oil

16 ounces fresh baby bella mushrooms, sliced

¾ teaspoon salt

Freshly ground black pepper

½ teaspoon garlic powder

½ teaspoon parsley flakes

¼ cup all-purpose flour

2 cups chicken broth (or beef/vegetable stock)

Directions

Preheat oven to 350° F.

Combine the chicken meatloaf ingredients in a bowl and mix gently.

Form the mixture into a 2-pound loaf, place in a lightly greased loaf pan, and cover with foil.

Bake at 350° F for 65 minutes.

Meanwhile, to prepare the mushroom gravy, heat the oil in a medium-sized pot.

Once the oil is hot, stir in the sliced mushrooms. Season with salt, pepper, garlic powder, and parsley flakes. Cook over a medium flame for 10 to 15 minutes. Reduce heat to low, sprinkle the flour over the mushroom mixture, and pour the chicken broth. Stir to combine, making sure no lumps of flour remain. Simmer for 3 to 5 minutes until the mixture thickens.

Sweet and Savory Cranberry Chicken

Yield: 6 servings

This chicken is unique and fruity, with a tangy combination flavor that's similar to sweet and sour.

Ingredients

6 chicken bottoms, without skin

Cranberry Sauce

1 tablespoon vegetable oil

1 small onion, finely diced

1 clove garlic, minced

¼ cup sweet red wine

2 tablespoons balsamic vinegar

2 cups cranberries, fresh or frozen (thawed)

½ cup sugar

¼ teaspoon kosher salt

¼ teaspoon freshly ground black pepper

Directions

Preheat oven to 350° F.

In small saucepan, heat the oil over a high flame. Stir in the onion and garlic and sauté, stirring occasionally, for 5 to 7 minutes, until softened. Stir in the wine and balsamic vinegar, then boil for 5 minutes or until reduced to about 3 tablespoons.

Meanwhile, slice the cranberries in half. In a bowl, stir together the cranberries, sugar, salt and pepper.

Add the cranberries to the reduced onion mixture. Bring to a boil and cook, stirring often, for 8 to 10 minutes or until the cranberries are tender and the sauce is thick.

Place the chicken bottoms in a roaster-size pan. Pour the cranberry sauce over the chicken and cover the pan with foil.

Bake at 350° F for 1½ hours, then uncover and bake for an additional 15 to 20 minutes.

E-Z P-Z Breaded Chicken

Yield: 6 servings

This is a really simple recipe, yet still delicious and appreciated every time, which is why I have included it here.

Ingredients

6 skinless chicken bottoms

1 recipe Garlic Mayo

1½–2 cups cornflake crumbs

Directions

Preheat oven to 350° F.

Generously coat the chicken bottoms with Garlic Mayo on all sides. Then bread the chicken with the cornflakes crumbs on all sides. Place in a 9" x 13" or roasting pan and cover.

Bake at 350° F for 1½ hours, covered.

Uncover and increase the oven temperature to 375° F. Bake uncovered for an additional 15 to 20 minutes.

Garlic Mayo Recipe

1 cup mayonnaise

½ teaspoon chili powder (optional)

1 clove garlic, crushed

Combine the ingredients together and mix well to incorporate.

Chicken Liver

Yield: 4–6 servings

If you are like me and like liver, you know that with liver, less is more. I remember one attempt at impressing my Shabbos guests: I made a whole complicated recipe for liver cooked in a pepper sauce concoction. To make a long story short, everyone asked me if I had some regular liver...

Liver doesn't need much, and the trick to cooking liver is not over-cooking it. Our liver comes already broiled, so we don't really have to cook it for long. I sauté the onions first, low and slow, so they are super soft; then I add the flavoring and throw in the liver for just a few minutes, so that the liver remains tender.

I usually keep the spices and flavors pretty basic. Sometimes I'll add a dash of balsamic vinegar or dry red wine, to be fancy.

Ingredients

½ cup oil

2 large onions, sliced

1–2 tablespoons balsamic vinegar (optional)

½ teaspoon paprika

½ teaspoon onion powder

½ teaspoon sugar

pinch of salt

pinch of black pepper

1½ pounds broiled chicken livers

Directions

Heat the oil in a pan over a high flame. Add the onions and lower the heat to medium. Sauté the onions for a good 10 minutes or so, stirring intermittently until the onions are soft and translucent.

Add the balsamic vinegar, paprika, onion powder, sugar, salt, and pepper. Mix everything together with the onions and cook for an additional 5 minutes over medium-low heat.

Add in the chicken livers and toss well with the onion mixture to fully combine all flavors. Cook for an additional 3 minutes. Remove from heat and don't overcook.

Marinated Turkey London Broil

Yield: 4 servings

Turkey London broil is a cut from the breast—a heavy, filling meat. When done right, it can be very juicy as well! This recipe yields a super tender and flavorful dish.

Short on Time:

If it's one of those days … don't fret! It's not essential to marinate the turkey for hours. You can always just rub on the spices and broil the turkey right then and there. (Just keep in mind that marinating it will result in a softer texture.)

Ingredients

2 (1–1¼" thick) pieces turkey London broil (total weight 3 pounds)

Marinade

3 tablespoons soy sauce

2 teaspoons lemon juice

1 teaspoon balsamic vinegar

1 teaspoon mustard

2 cloves garlic, crushed

1 teaspoon parsley flakes

1 teaspoon dried basil

1 teaspoon oregano

1 tablespoon brown sugar

dash of salt

dash of black pepper

Directions

Combine the marinade ingredients in a small bowl. Rub the mixture all over the turkey London broil. Place the turkey and remaining marinade in a covered dish or heavy-duty Ziploc bag and marinate in the refrigerator for at least 3 hours (up to overnight).

Preheat oven to broil.

Place the turkey London broil on a lined baking sheet. Broil on high for 10 minutes.

Flip the pieces of turkey over and broil for an additional 10 minutes, or until cooked through.

Cut each piece of turkey into slices and serve immediately.

Meat

When it comes to roast recipes, people are always asking for recipes for specific cuts: "Do you have a good recipe for Delmonico? A minute roast recipe?"

I want to clarify that all roast recipes can be used for any type of roast. Find a recipe with flavors you like, and then simply adjust the cooking temperature and time as needed for that particular cut.

There are fattier cuts of meat, like second-cut brisket and all those that come from the chuck, including French roast, Delmonico roast, chuck eye, etc. These are all fattier pieces, therefore you can cook them at a higher heat (like 325° F) for one hour per pound. Then there are the dryer cuts, like first-cut brisket and those that come from the shoulder, like silvertip roast. These cuts are leaner, and therefore they need to be cooked at a lower heat (usually 275° F) for one hour per pound.

Meatballs with Marsala Mushroom Sauce

Yield: 10–12 large meatballs

We often associate meatballs with a casual dinner, but these meatballs with Marsala mushroom sauce are a different story entirely. They are gourmet and elegant, perfect for Shabbos and Yom Tov, and so rich in flavor. When I make them for Yom Tov or a special supper, I like to serve them over fluffy mashed potatoes.

Ingredients

Meatballs

1½ pounds ground beef chuck

⅓ cup breadcrumbs

1 large egg, lightly beaten

½ cup chicken broth

¼ teaspoon freshly ground pepper

Mushroom Sauce

2 tablespoons oil

12 ounces mixed mushrooms, sliced

½ teaspoon salt

pepper

1 tablespoon all-purpose flour

1 cup dry Marsala wine

1 cup chicken broth

Fluffy Mashed Potatoes

1½ pounds Yukon Gold potatoes, peeled and cut into 1-inch chunks

4 tablespoons oil

½ cup chicken broth

Kosher salt

pepper

Directions

Meatballs: Preheat the broiler.

Place the meatball ingredients in a medium bowl, and mix with your hands until combined.

Form into 12 meatballs (approximately 2 inches each) and arrange on a rimmed baking sheet.

Broil for 7 minutes, until browned, but not fully cooked.

Marsala Mushroom Sauce: Heat the oil in a large pot over high heat, then add the mushrooms, salt and a few grinds of pepper. Cook, stirring, until the mushrooms are softened (about 8 minutes).

Sprinkle in the flour and stir to coat. Stir in the wine and bring to a boil.

Add the chicken broth and return to a boil, then reduce heat to medium-high and add the meatballs.

Simmer, stirring occasionally, for 2 to 4 minutes, until the sauce is nicely thickened.

Fluffy Mashed Potatoes: Place the potatoes in a saucepan and add water to cover by 1 inch; season with salt. Bring to a boil, then reduce to a simmer; cook until tender (about 20 minutes).

Drain and return to the saucepan to mash. Add the oil and chicken broth to the potatoes and mash. Season with salt and pepper.

Note: I've frozen the meatballs together with the mushroom sauce. It defrosted and re-warmed beautifully and was delicious!

RAIZY FRIED

BBQ Pulled Brisket

Here's my popular BBQ pulled brisket recipe. It doesn't use BBQ sauce, but all the flavors in the recipe create your very own BBQ-like sauce. I love how easy this recipe is—no pots, no sauce to cook up. Simply mix the ingredients, pour over your meat, and pop into the oven.

This brisket recipe is super versatile—you can slice it or pull it. The pulled brisket is delicious for Shabbos or every day: serve it in crispy tacos, use it to top burgers or pizza flatbreads, drizzle it with Caesar dressing, or bake it in a fluffy babka dough (*see next page*).

Whichever way you serve it, this pulled brisket is far better than the one at your favorite restaurant.

Ingredients

2 pounds second-cut brisket

Sauce

1 cup ketchup

½ cup water

¼ cup apple cider vinegar

2½ tablespoons sugar

2½ tablespoons light brown sugar

¼ teaspoon black pepper

½ teaspoon onion powder

1½ teaspoons lemon juice

1½ teaspoons (fish-free) Worcestershire sauce

Directions

Preheat oven to 350° F.

Score the brisket diagonally on both sides. Place the brisket in a 9" x 13" pan.

In a small bowl, whisk together all the sauce ingredients. Pour the sauce over the meat and cover the pan.

Bake at 350° F for 2½ hours, or until very tender. When fully cooked, use 2 forks to pull the brisket apart in the pan.

Brisket Babka

Yield: 2 babkas (baked in 3-pound loaf pans)

A savory babka: pockets of tasty brisket encased in fluffy challah-like dough, accented with garlic mayo—this recipe is something special!

Ingredients

1 (3–4 pound) first- or second-cut brisket, cooked and pulled *(see previous page)*

Babka Dough

4¾ cups flour

1 tablespoon sugar

2 teaspoons salt

1 stick margarine

2 eggs

¼ cup oil

1 ounce (3⅓ tablespoons) active dry yeast, dissolved in 1 cup warm water

½ cup seltzer

1 recipe Garlic Mayo *(see p. 140)*

2 eggs, beaten

Directions

Preheat oven to 350° F.

Using a mixer fitted with the dough hook, mix the dough for a good 10 minutes.

Add a bit more flour if the dough is sticky.

Divide the dough into 4 even portions. Roll out each portion of dough and smear with a generous layer of Garlic Mayo, then top with pulled brisket. Roll up jelly-roll style.

Take 2 rolls and twist them to form a babka. Place each babka in a 3-pound loaf pan and brush with beaten egg.

Bake at 350° F for 1 hour.

Note: To prepare in advance, cook the brisket, make the dough, form the babka, and place it in a disposable pan, ready to go, and then freeze it unbaked. Remove it from the freezer on Erev Shabbos or Yom Tov to defrost and bake, so it's perfectly fresh!

Coffee Garlic French Roast

Yield: approximately 6 servings

This recipe is the one that I make when I don't have any extra time to marinate the meat. The eclectic ingredient list melds beautifully, and the Coke is actually there for a very good reason—the acid in Coke tenderizes the meat as it cooks, giving you superb results in a fraction of the time.

Ingredients

1 (3-pound) French roast

8 cloves fresh garlic, crushed

2 teaspoons coffee granules, dissolved in 1 teaspoon hot water

¼ cup olive oil

1 tablespoon brown sugar

½ teaspoon salt

¼–½ teaspoon freshly ground black pepper

½ cup Coke

Directions

Preheat oven to 350° F.

In a small bowl, combine the crushed garlic, coffee mixture, oil, brown sugar, salt, and pepper. Rub the mixture all over the roast and place in a 9" x 13" pan.

Broil the roast on high for 5 minutes, uncovered.

Remove the pan from the oven, and preheat oven to 350° F.

Pour the soda over the roast and cover the pan tightly with foil.

Return the pan to the oven and bake at 350° F for 3 hours.

Remove from oven and allow to cool.

Once cooled, slice the roast and season with additional freshly ground black pepper, if needed.

The Butcher's French Roast

Yield: 8–10 servings

This is our favorite roast recipe, which we make over and over again. The combination of tomatoes, duck sauce, and wine is incredible.

Ingredients

2 onions, sliced into rings

2 tomatoes, sliced into rings

1 (5-pound) French roast (or square cut roast)

1½ cups duck sauce

1½ cups dry red wine

1 tablespoon onion powder

2 teaspoons garlic powder

2 teaspoons paprika

Salt

Freshly ground black pepper

Directions

Place half the onions and half the tomatoes in a large roasting pan. Place the roast on top, and cover with the remaining tomatoes and onions, duck sauce, wine, and spices.

Cover the pan and refrigerate for at least 2 hours or (even better) overnight.

Preheat oven to 375° F.

Bring the roast to room temperature.

Bake, covered, at 375° F for about 3 hours and 15 minutes, until tender when pierced with a fork. Remove from oven and allow to cool.

Transfer to a cutting board. Using a sharp knife, cut thin slices across the grain.

Place the slices on a serving plate and dress with the sauce.

Tip: I like a thicker sauce, so I remove the onions, tomatoes, and a bit of the liquid from the pan and blend it into a sauce.

Classic Roast

Yield: approximately 8 servings

One of our all-time favorite roast recipes: not too sweet, not too plain—just perfect.
Best served with mashed potatoes and plenty of gravy!

Ingredients

1 (4-pound) Delmonico or
French roast

2 onions, cut in rings

2 cups red wine

¼ cup soy sauce

¼–½ cup firmly packed
brown sugar

4 tablespoons olive oil

6 cloves garlic, crushed

2 tablespoons onion powder

1 tablespoon salt

1½ teaspoons freshly ground
black pepper

Directions

Place the sliced onions at the bottom of a
9" x 13" pan. Place the roast on top of the
onions.

In a medium bowl, whisk together all
the other ingredients, then pour over the
roast. Cover and allow to marinate in the
refrigerator, preferably overnight.

Preheat oven to 325° F.

Bake for 1 hour per pound, covered.

Super Soft Minute Steak

Yield: 12 slices

Many don't like making minute steak, because they are bothered by the vein in the center of the cut. This recipe performs some kind of magic … I never had minute steak this soft, until I tasted this recipe one Yom Tov at my mother's.

✓ super-soft results

✓ clean ingredients

✓ easy recipe

✓ *heimishe* taste everyone will love

Ingredients

12 (½-inch thick) slices
  minute steak

Sauce

2 Spanish onions, cut into
  quarters

½ cup oil

2 cups water

1 teaspoon salt

dash of freshly ground black
  pepper

1½ tablespoons paprika

4–5 cloves fresh garlic

Directions

Preheat oven to 350° F.

Place the sauce ingredients in a pot, cover, and cook over medium heat until the onions are soft (about 50 minutes). Once the onions are soft, use an immersion blender to blend the sauce ingredients together until you have a creamy consistency.

Lay the slices of meat flat in a pan, pour the sauce over the meat, and cover the pan tightly.

Bake at 350° F for 3 to 3½ hours.

Slow-Cooked Roast

Yield: approximately 8 servings

Easy as pie. Soft like butter. This simple, Slow-Cooked Roast is definitely worth a try!

Ingredients

2 onions, sliced

1 (4-pound) chuck eye roast or Delmonico roast

1 teaspoon kosher salt

¾ teaspoon freshly ground black pepper

3 ripe tomatoes, diced

4 cloves garlic, crushed

Directions

Place the sliced onions in a Crock-Pot and top with the roast. Season the roast with salt and pepper. Pour the diced tomatoes and garlic over the roast.

Cover and cook on high for 1 hour.

Reduce heat to low and cook for an additional 9 hours.

Once the roast is done cooking, transfer all the onions and tomatoes to a separate bowl or container, add about ¼ cup of the liquid, and blend using an immersion blender to yield a nice, thick gravy.

Kugels & Sides

Simple Potato Kugel

Yield: 1 (9" x 13") pan

Ahh ... Potato kugel is one of the all-time *heimishe* Comfort Foods! (My family pronounces it *"kigel."*)

Here is the easiest, simplest, no-fail potato kugel recipe.

While I have many different recipes for different versions of potato kugel, I knew that I had to include the simplest one in my book, because so many are intimidated by potato kugel—for no good reason.

Potato kugel doesn't need to be complicated to be delicious.

The first potato kugel is so easy, I end up making it most often. The recipe has got no onions, no need to heat oil, and it's yummy! Try it and you'll see.

Ingredients

10 Yukon Gold potatoes, peeled

6 eggs

¾ cup oil

½ cup unflavored seltzer or water

2 teaspoons salt

½–1 teaspoon black pepper

Directions

Preheat oven to 450° F.

In the bowl of a food processor fitted with the S-blade, combine the eggs, oil, seltzer, salt, and pepper.

Once the mixture is combined, pour it into a 9" x 13" pan.

Remove the S-blade and fit the food processor with either the "C" fine shredding blade or "E" grating blade (depending on how you like your kugel, shredded or grated).

Shred or grate the potatoes, then add them to the pan and mix well with the egg mixture already in the pan.

Bake uncovered at 450° F for 1 hour. Reduce the oven temperature to 350° F and bake for another hour.

Potato Kugel Notes and Hacks

Use Seltzer: Seltzer instead of water gives potato kugel an incredibly fluffy texture.

Type of Potatoes: Use Idaho potatoes or Yukon Gold Potatoes. They each taste very different; I like both, but I prefer the rich flavor and creamy texture you get from Yukon Gold potatoes.

Hack: For potatoes to peel easily, chill the potatoes before peeling in a bowl of cold water. Afterward, they'll peel 1-2-3.

Super Time Hack: In the Simple Potato Kugel recipe, if you're using Yukon Gold potatoes, and you're terribly short on time, you don't even have to peel them. Just clean them very well and grate or shred them—you won't taste the peels at all.

Check the directions for more hacks I use when I'm whipping up my potato kugel. I take advantage of my food processor and combine everything in the pan. No separate bowl needed!

Gourmet Potato Kugel

Yield: 1 (9" x 13") pan

This kugel is fancier—more "gourmet," as I call it. It's more of a *patchke* and incredibly tasty and special. This recipe comes from Gitty Frankel, an uber-talented personal chef.

My family is very picky when it comes to eating storebought food, especially for Shabbos. We were overjoyed when we tried Gitty's delicious *heimishe* food. Everything Gitty makes is delicious! She uses wholesome ingredients and just the right balance of flavors. Gitty is generous and *"geshikt,"* as we say in Yiddish; she packages the food neatly and labels her foil pan covers with a handwritten *"Lekoved Shabbos Kodesh."*

Ingredients

4 Idaho potatoes (loose)

5 Yukon Gold* potatoes

9 eggs

1 large Spanish onion

1 cup oil

1 cup hot water

1 tablespoon salt

Black pepper

White pepper

Directions

Preheat oven to 550° F.

Peel the potatoes and place in cold water.

Heat the oil in a 9" x 13" pan over a medium flame until hot, then remove from heat and set aside.

Using a (Braun) food processor fitted with the S-blade, purée the onion completely. Add the eggs and pulse until combined. Transfer into a large bowl.

Using the "C" fine shredding blade, shred half the potatoes. Transfer to the bowl.

Using the "E" grating blade, grate the other half of the potatoes. Add the grated potatoes, hot water, and seasonings to the mixture in the bowl and mix well. Carefully, while stirring, add the hot oil.

*Gitty prefers to use Green Giant's proprietary variety of Yukon Gold potatoes, sold as Klondike Goldust.

Spray the pan with cooking oil spray. Pour the kugel mixture into the pan.

Bake at 550° F for 25 minutes, then lower the oven temperature to 475° F and bake for 40 minutes.

Lower the oven temperature once more, to 350° F, and bake for approximately 45 minutes.

Mini Gourmet Potato Kugel

Yield: 1 (4" x 6") pan

This is a miniature version of the kugel above, perfect for one or two.

Ingredients

2 Yukon Gold potatoes

1 Idaho potato

1 onion

3 eggs

¼ cup oil, heated

⅓ cup hot water

1 teaspoon salt

Pinch pepper

Directions

Following the directions above, prepare the kugel mixture.

Spray a 4" x 6" pan with cooking oil spray. Pour the kugel mixture into the pan.

Bake at 550° F for 15 minutes, and then at 350° F for approximately 40 minutes.

Yapchik

Yield: 1 (9" x 13") pan

There are two kinds of yapchik: one that looks like a regular kugel, but with chunks of meat; and then there's the one I love! Where it's all one big mush, and you've got pieces of tasty meat in every bite!

Ingredients

8 large russet potatoes, peeled and rinsed

1 Spanish onion

6 eggs

1 cup oil

1½ tablespoons salt

¼ teaspoon freshly ground black pepper

1½ pounds second-cut brisket or kolichel, cubed

Directions

Preheat oven to 425° F.

Using a food processor fitted with the "E" grating blade, grate the potatoes and onion, then transfer to a large bowl or pan.

Using the S-blade, process the eggs, oil, salt and pepper. Then add the egg mixture to the bowl or pan with the grated potatoes. Add the cubed meat to the bowl, and mix everything well.

Transfer to a 9" x 13" pan.

Bake uncovered at 425° F for 1½ hours.

Reduce oven temperature to 225° F, cover the baking pan tightly with heavy duty foil (or doubled regular foil) and bake for an additional 6 hours.

Once fully cooked, remove the kugel from the oven. Break open the top layer of the kugel and mix well with a fork, to pull the meat apart and combine all the soft meat and potatoes into one delicious mush.

Serve hot.

Apple Cranberry Crumb Kugel

Yield: 2 medium (3-pound) loaf pans

Whenever I make this kugel, it's enjoyed to the last crumb!

Now here is the second-best part of this recipe (the first is its deliciousness!): If you prepare the full crumb recipe, even when you just want one kugel, you'll always have a batch of crumbs in the freezer for another week. Then, when a lazy (or busy!) week comes around, all you need to do is prepare the apples, take out the crumbs, put it together, and bake.

Ingredients

Crumbs

4½ cups flour

1½ cups sugar

1 cup oil

1½ teaspoons baking powder

1 tablespoon vanilla sugar

2 eggs

Filling

6–8 Cortland apples, peeled and thinly sliced

2 tablespoons vanilla sugar

¼ cup sugar

2 (16-ounce) cans jellied cranberries

Directions

Preheat oven to 350° F.

Using a mixer, mix together all the crumb ingredients until combined into a crumby mixture.

To prepare the filling, combine the sliced apples with the sugars.

To assemble, place a layer of crumbs in each loaf pan, followed by a layer of apples. Then spread a can of jellied cranberries (without liquid) on top of the apple layer (one can per pan). Finish off with a generous additional layer of the crumb mixture.

Bake at 350° F for 55–65 minutes, until the top is crispy and golden. (You don't want the top to be mushy or soggy, the crunchy crumby top is the best part!)

Serve warm or at room temperature.

Note: If you are making one kugel and freezing half the crumbs, remember to halve the apple filling recipe.

Tip: For best results, use a mandoline to get perfectly thin slices of apple.

Babbie's Apple Cake

Yield: 1 (3-pound) loaf cake

This is my grandmother's apple cake recipe, which she makes every week *lekoved Shabbos*. This apple cake is so "regular," yet it elevates the Shabbos meal. With ribbons of thinly sliced apples threaded between layers of cake, this cake is as cozy-tasting as can be!

Ingredients

4 eggs

1 cup sugar

1 teaspoon vanilla sugar

⅓ cup oil

¾ teaspoon baking powder

1 cup all-purpose flour

2 yellow apples, peeled and finely sliced

2 Red Delicious apples, peeled and finely sliced

Directions

Preheat oven to 350° F. Line a 3-pound loaf pan with parchment paper.

Using a mixer, beat the eggs with the sugars. Add in the oil and baking powder and mix together. Lastly, add the flour and mix until well combined.

Layer the batter and the apples inside the lined loaf pan: Spoon a bit of the batter, then add some slices of apples. Keep repeating, alternating batter and apples, until the pan is full. The top layer should be a combination of apples and batter, with a bit more batter.

Bake at 350° F for 1 hour.

Note: To slice the apples as finely as needed, I use a mandolin.

Challah Kugel

Yield: 1 (9" x 13") pan

This is a great way to use leftover challah, but if you don't have leftover challah, it's worth buying a bakery challah to try it!

Ingredients

1 large heimishe challah

5 eggs

1 cup oil

1 cup sugar

2 tablespoons vanilla sugar

1 teaspoon cinnamon

4 Granny Smith green apples,
   peeled and finely sliced

Sugar, for sprinkling

Directions

Preheat oven to 350° F.

Soak the challah in water and squeeze it out. Use only the soft part of the challah; discard the crust.

In a large bowl, mash the challah. Using an electric mixer, mix the mashed challah with the rest of the ingredients.

Place the mixture in a lined or greased 9" x 13" pan. Sprinkle some sugar on top.

Bake at 350° F for 1 hour and 45 minutes.

Best served warm.

Nut Lukshen Kugel

Yield: 2 (3-pound) loaf pans

It's not your typical lukshen kugel—it is very different: nutty, light and airy, and mildly sweet.

Ingredients

1 (10-ounce) bag medium egg noodles (also called kugel noodles)

6 eggs, separated

¾ cup sugar

1 tablespoon vanilla sugar

1 tablespoon oil

2 tablespoons heavy sweet red wine

¾ cup ground walnuts

Directions

Preheat oven to 350° F. Line two (3-pound) loaf pans with parchment paper.

Cook the noodles according to the package directions.

Using an electric mixer, beat the egg whites with the sugar until it forms stiff peaks.

In a separate bowl, combine the yolks with the vanilla sugar, oil, wine and walnuts.

Gently fold the yolk mixture into the snow and then combine well with the cooked noodles.

Divide the mixture evenly between the prepared pans.

Bake uncovered at 350° F for 50 minutes.

Best served warm.

Yerushalmi Kugel

Yield: 1 (9") round pan

This is my very talented friend Ruth's recipe. You'll notice several techniques, like using a bit of the pasta water and whipping the eggs really well, that make this kugel incredibly moist and fluffy! This is a really good Yerushalmi kugel—it's got the browned sugar and the pepper, but what makes this even better, is that it's LIGHT! This Yerushalmi kugel is delightful, just like Ruth herself.

Ingredients

- 1 (10-ounce) bag fine egg noodles
- 1½ cups sugar
- ½ cup oil
- 2 teaspoons kosher salt
- 2 teaspoons freshly ground black pepper
- 8 eggs

Directions

Preheat oven to 350° F.

Cook the pasta according to the directions on the package. When the pasta is done cooking, reserve ½ cup of the pasta water, and set aside. Drain the rest of the pasta; do not rinse.

In a separate pot, over medium–high heat, melt the sugar and oil together, stirring constantly for 10 to 15 minutes, until the mixture is a deep caramel.

Note: Don't let the sugar caramelize for too long, as it can get bitter if it gets too dark.

Turn off the heat and let cool for 6–8 minutes.

Add the cooked pasta to the pot with the caramelized mixture, and mix gently to combine. Add the salt and pepper, and set aside.

In a large bowl, beat the eggs very well. Add the reserved pasta water and mix to incorporate.

In a large bowl, combine the pasta mixture with the egg mixture.

Grease a 9" round pan well. Pour the whole mixture into the prepared pan. Cover the pan with foil.

Bake at 350° F for 40 minutes. Uncover and bake for an additional 25 minutes.

Best served warm.

Ferfel • פערפל

Yield: approximately 6 servings

My mother makes toasted, golden brown ferfel. When I saw pale ferfel for the first time, I assumed the cook simply didn't know how to cook it. Yet after eating ferfel at several places other than my home, I discovered there were various kinds of ferfel … and have come to appreciate the moist, pale version of ferfel as well.

Nonetheless, I still like using the pre-toasted ferfel. You can toast ferfel by sautéing it in 2 tablespoons vegetable oil for a couple of minutes, until browned.

Tips to ensure that your ferfel doesn't dry out or clump up:

• If you're cooking ferfel for Shabbos, undercook it a bit or add extra hot water on the top before placing it on your hot plate or in your oven for Shabbos.

• I don't put my ferfel directly on the hot plate—I set it up on an overturned cupcake tin. This way it remains warm, but doesn't dry out.

• Another great tip to keep ferfel moist is to mix in approximately 2 tablespoons vegetable oil after it's done cooking.

Ingredients

1 (10 ounce) package ferfel

2 tablespoons canola oil

½ teaspoon paprika

1 teaspoon onion powder

½ teaspoon garlic powder

½ teaspoon salt

¼ teaspoon freshly ground
   black pepper

Boiling water

Directions

Heat the oil in a saucepan over a high flame. When the oil is hot, add the ferfel and sauté for a minute or two. Once browned, season the ferfel with the spices. Cover the ferfel well with boiling hot water. Then cover the pot and allow to simmer for 5 minutes, or until the ferfel is cooked.

Zeese Mayeren
זיסע מייערן

Yield: 4–6 servings

Sweet carrots, otherwise known as *"tzimmes,"* are sliced carrots cooked in sugar. For many, this dish is associated with Rosh Hashanah, but we have a *minhag* to eat a bit every Friday night with the main course.

Ingredients

2 thick carrots, peeled and thinly sliced

½ cup sugar

1 tablespoon canola oil

½ teaspoon salt

Directions

Place the sliced carrots in a small saucepan, and cover with water. Add the sugar and the oil, then cover the pot and bring to a boil. Once bubbling, reduce heat to low and cook for about 45 minutes, simmering on a low flame.

Desserts

Apple Compote

Yield: approximately 7 (2-pound) containers

Traditional Apple Compote is what I serve on Friday Night. It's simple: literally apples and water. The trick is using the right apples, and letting it cook low and slow ... Of course, you can add sugar, but I don't find that it's necessary—if you choose the right sweet apples and you cook them long enough, the compote comes out sweet as sugar. When I do add sweetener, I add a little honey or vanilla sugar. Yellow apples together with a bit of vanilla sugar is a great combination!

Let's talk about apples, because choosing the right apple can make or break a recipe. Some of the most popular apples for cooking and baking are Granny Smith, Golden Delicious, Cortland, Fuji and Honeycrisp, though there are hundreds of types of apples around the world.

Granny Smith apples are great for cooking and baking, as they are crisp and hold their shape beautifully, but they are tart. Cortland apples are slighty softer and sweeter, and cook pretty well too. My personal favorites to use for compote are the Golden Delicious yellow apples—they are sweet, with a rich mellow flavor, and have the right body when cooked.

Ingredients

20–24 Golden Delicious yellow apples, peeled and cubed

¼ cup vanilla sugar (optional)

2–3 cups black grapes, in mesh cooking bag, for color (optional)

Directions

Place the cubed apples and the mesh bag with grapes (if desired) in an 8-quart pot. Sprinkle with vanilla sugar and cover with water.

Cover the pot and bring to a boil. Once bubbling, reduce heat to medium-low and cook for about 1 hour.

Tip: To add a nice pink color to the compote, place some black grapes in a mesh cooking bag and cook them with the apples.

Apple Cranberry Compote

Yield: 6–8 servings

I often cook the apples with complementary seasonal fruit, such as plums, peaches, and pineapples. This, and the following recipe, are my favorite combinations.

Ingredients

8 apples, peeled and cubed

1 cup fresh cranberries

½ cup honey

3 cinnamon sticks

Directions

Follow the directions on page 186.

Puréed Apple Pineapple Compote

Yield: approximately 8 servings

The idea of adding pineapple to compote comes from my Aunt Surie. If you were to google the word *"balabusta,"* her name would pop up. (If she were on the Internet, that is!)

She's the one who told me about including cooked pineapple in her compote. I tried it, and it tastes so tropical and fresh! (She says mango with yellow apples is amazing too.)

There's no sugar needed when you use yellow apples and bake for two hours—with the acidity of the pineapple, it's just delicious!

Amazingly, there are only two ingredients! (Okay, three if you count the water.)

Ingredients

8–10 yellow apples, peeled and cubed

1 fresh pineapple, sliced or cut into chunks

Directions

Cook: Place the apples and fresh pineapple into a pot. Fill with water to cover the fruit. Cover the pot and cook over low heat for 2 hours.

Bake: Preheat oven to 350° F. Place the apples and fresh pineapple into a deep 9" x 13" pan.

Fill with water to cover the fruit. Cover with foil and bake at 350° F for 2 hours.

After the compote is cooked, remove the pineapples from the pot or pan and transfer to a separate bowl. Blend using an immersion blender.

Pour the pineapple purée back into the pot or pan and mix the apples and pineapple together.

Serve chilled.

Pear 4 Ways

Juicy, soft, and sweet—pears are such a delicious fruit. It can be overwhelming, though, deciding which pear to buy from the vast variety in the fruit store. Especially when cooking or baking pears, you want to choose the right ones that will hold their shape.

Popular pears for that purpose are the Bosc and Anjou pears. I often choose the Bosc pears, because they are wonderfully crisp and have a delicate, sweet flavor that embodies the stereotypical flavor of a pear perfectly.

Cooked Pears in Wine with Strawberry Sauce

Yield: 8 servings

These elegant pears are simple to make and only require a few minutes of prep, but the results are sensational. A dessert like this makes a stunning finale to any special meal.

This recipe can be made well ahead of time: Cooked pears can be kept in an airtight container in the fridge for up to a week, and the same is true of the blended strawberry sauce. Store each separately, and combine just before serving.

Ingredients

8 Bosc pears, peeled

2 cups sweet red wine

Water

8 ounces frozen strawberries

¼ cup confectioners' sugar

¼ cup orange juice

Fresh mint leaves, as a
   garnish (optional)

Directions

In an 8-quart pot, place the peeled pears upright at the bottom of the pot. Add the 2 cups of wine and fill with water, until the pears are well covered.

Bring to a boil, then cook over medium heat for 35 minutes, until the pears are soft, yet still firm.

Remove from heat and allow the pears to cool in the pot before transferring them.

In a bowl, combine the strawberries, sugar, and orange juice. Using an immersion blender, blend until smooth.

Serve the pears at room temperature. To serve, place a pear upright on a plate and top with strawberry sauce.

Note: Level the bottom of each pear, so it will sit nicely on the plate.

Baked Pears with Honey and Cinnamon

Yield: 6 servings

Here's a recipe to add to your go-to list: easy enough to pull off for a Tuesday night dinner, but special enough to serve on Shabbos to guests. This impressive dessert is a hit at my house. It's fast, easy, and delicious! Most of all, I love the rustic look of this dessert.

Ingredients

3 Bosc pears, unpeeled and halved

¾ cup shelled walnuts

3 tablespoons honey

1 teaspoon cinnamon

Directions

Preheat oven to 350° F.

Scoop the center seeds out of the pears.

Level the bottom edge of each pear, so it will sit nicely on the plate.

Fill the scooped-out cavities with a bit of walnuts.

Drizzle with honey (approximately ½ teaspoon per pear) and season generously with cinnamon.

Bake at 350° F for 30 to 35 minutes, or until tender (test with fork).

Sautéed Pears in Honey Syrup

Yield: 4 servings

This cozy dessert is a honey of a salute to the awesome pear, with plenty of "wow" factors. If you want to take it up a notch, this pairs beautifully with vanilla ice cream. Drizzle the syrup on top of the ice cream, and you're in business.

Ingredients

3 Bosc pears, unpeeled and quartered

2 tablespoons canola oil

½ cup mild honey

1½ tablespoons lemon juice

Directions

Heat a pan, then add the oil, then the pears. Sauté on one cut side for 6 minutes, then flip over onto the other side for another minute.

Add the honey and cook for 3 minutes, until well glazed. Add the lemon juice and cook for another 2 minutes.

Plate the pears, and drizzle the sauce on top.

Quick Tip: When measuring honey or any other sticky ingredient, first spray the measuring cup or spoon with oil spray, then put in the honey. The honey will slide right out, instead of sticking to the utensil.

Puréed Pear Compote

Yield: approximately 8–10 servings

A refreshing, smooth dessert that will wash away any savory aftertaste, leaving only sweet notes and sweet memories of a great meal.

Ingredients

15 Anjou pears, peeled and quartered

1 (16-ounce) bag frozen rhubarb

1 cup sugar

1 bunch black grapes, in mesh cooking bag, for color (optional)

Kiwi, sliced, as a garnish (optional)

Directions

Place the pears, rhubarb, sugar, and grapes in a 6-quart pot and cover with water. Cover the pot, bring to a boil, and cook for about 15 minutes.

Reduce heat to medium-low and cook for 1 hour, until the pears are soft.

Remove 4 cups of the liquid and set aside. Remove the mesh bags with the grapes and discard. Using an immersion blender, purée the remaining liquid and cooked fruit.

Note: Before blending the pears, I remove some of the liquid and set it aside, because I prefer a thicker consistency for the purée. Don't discard the pear liquid, though— refrigerate it and enjoy on its own as a super-refreshing drink. My treat!

Pomme au Chocolat

Yield: 8 servings

Warm baked apple—only better!

These baked apples are encased in flaky dough and have got a sweet surprise in their core—runny, warm chocolate!

What could be better?

Ingredients

4 Cortland apples, peeled, halved, and cored

8 squares good quality chocolate

8 (4½") squares puff pastry, thawed

¼ cup canola oil

3 tablespoons sugar

¼ teaspoon cinnamon

Confectioners' sugar, for sprinkling

Directions

Preheat oven to 400° F. Line a baking sheet with parchment paper.

In a small bowl, combine the oil, cinnamon and sugar.

Brush the halved and cored apples with the oil and sugar mixture.

Place the coated apples on the prepared baking sheet, with the cavity facing up. Place a square of chocolate inside each cavity. (If the chocolate doesn't fit, break it in half and insert both pieces.)

Place a square of thawed pastry over each apple to cover the cavity with the chocolate. Fold the edges of puff pastry over the sides, wrapping it around the apples.

Bake at 400° F for 20 to 22 minutes, until the apples are soft but firm, and the puff pastry is golden.

Sprinkle with confectioners' sugar and serve immediately.

Refreshing "Whipped" Fruit Cup

Yield: approximately 6–8 servings

This is one of those desserts that although it's rather typical and oh-so-easy, it'll go every time. Plates licked clean, requests for more … Every time.

Ingredients

1 (16-ounce) package frozen strawberries

½ (20-ounce) can pineapple tidbits

1 (11-ounce) can mandarin oranges

1 (16-ounce) container whipped topping

Directions

Using an immersion blender, blend the strawberries. Combine with the topping (no need to whip it up!).

Add the pineapples and mandarin oranges, including the liquid from each, and mix to combine.

Refrigerate until ready to serve.

Upside-Down Peach Cupcakes

Yield: approximately 22 medium cupcakes

Who doesn't just love summer and all the juicy fruit that come with it?

These upside-down peach cupcakes are so sweet and fluffy—they make a great dessert on their own. I like to serve them warm with a scoop of vanilla ice cream to take things up a notch.

Ingredients

3–4 peaches, ripe but firm, thinly sliced

Cupcakes

¾ **cup sugar**

3 eggs

½ **cup orange juice**

1 cup oil

2 cups Quality All-Purpose Cake Flour

1 tablespoon baking powder

1 teaspoon lemon extract

Syrup

½ **stick margarine**

½ **cup firmly packed light brown sugar**

Directions

Preheat oven to 350° F.

Using a mixer, beat the sugar and eggs together, then mix in the rest of the cake ingredients, adding one ingredient at a time.

In a small saucepan over high heat, melt the margarine. Reduce heat to low and add the brown sugar. Whisk well until it forms a caramelized light syrup texture.

Spray the muffin tins with cooking oil spray. Place 1 teaspoon of the brown sugar mixture in each cavity. Arrange 4 slices of peach, lying flat on top of the brown sugar, in each cavity. Using a spoon, fill the cavity two-thirds full with the batter.

Bake at 350° F for 20 to 25 minutes.

Remove from oven and allow to cool completely in the pan before turning over.

Once cooled, flip over the pan to release the cupcakes. If some don't come out right away, tap the top of the pan with a spoon.

Peanut Butter Mousse

Yield: approximately 3 (1-pound) containers

I've had a few versions of peanut butter mousse at several restaurants. There is just something about a simple, fluffy mousse that makes you drool for more. So I finally recreated it, and to my surprise, it was way easier than I thought it would be! It takes less than five minutes, and you've got a taste that's pretty close to gourmet!

This peanut butter mousse is rich, delicious, and so light. I love topping it with a mixture of crushed Viennese crunch and rice crispies.

There are so many ways you can present and plate this dessert. I love going all out and piping this mousse atop a Chocolate Chip Brownie (recipe on page 244) with a fresh fruit salsa at the side. For easy alternatives that can be prepped in advance and frozen, you can pipe the mousse into disposable mini-ware cups, or inside store-bought cannolis.

Ingredients

Mousse

1 (16-ounce) container whipped topping

5 tablespoons creamy peanut butter

3 tablespoons pure maple syrup

Crunch

1 cup rice crispies

5 Viennese crunch, crushed

½ cup mini chocolate chips (optional)

Directions

Beat the whipped topping until stiff peaks form. Then add the maple syrup and peanut butter and mix to combine. Do not over-mix.

Refrigerate the mousse in an airtight container until ready to serve.

Mix the rice crispies with the crushed Viennese crunch and chocolate chips.

To serve, spoon or pipe (I like using the star or round tip) some mousse into a small dish or mini-ware. Top with plenty of the crunch mixture.

Strawberry Shortcake

❧

Yield: 6–8 servings

This strawberry shortcake recipe is absolutely divine! I love a strawberry shortcake that uses real strawberries (as opposed to jam-like fillings). This particular vanilla cake is also a favorite, because it's very moist and fluffy, which makes it all come together beautifully.

I like to assemble strawberry shortcake before the meal (or before serving) in martini glasses—I think it makes such a statement! But if you're looking for something compact that you can prepare in advance, put them together in little mason jars—they are adorable! The assembled strawberry shortcakes can be refrigerated for 1 to 3 days in airtight jars.

Ingredients

Vanilla Cake

2½ cups Quality All-Purpose Cake Flour

1¾ cups sugar

1 tablespoon baking powder

¾ cup orange juice

¾ cup canola oil

2 teaspoons pure vanilla extract

4 large eggs

Whipped Cream

1 (16-ounce) container whipped topping

1 tablespoon sugar

2 teaspoons vanilla sugar

Strawberries

1 (16-ounce) container strawberries, sliced

¼ cup sugar

1 teaspoon lemon juice

Directions

Preheat oven to 325° F. Line a baking sheet with parchment paper.

Combine the cake ingredients in the bowl of an electric mixer and mix to incorporate.

Pour the batter onto the lined baking sheet.

Bake at 325° F for 25 to 30 minutes, until the cake is baked through, but still looks sticky and a bit moist on top.

Whip the topping and sugars together until stiff peaks form.

Toss the strawberries, sugar, and lemon juice in a bowl and allow to sit for about 20 minutes.

To assemble, cut circles of cake using a cookie cutter or glass. (The circles should be a bit smaller than your jar opening or cup.)

Then layer the cake, strawberries, and whip. Repeat the layers.

Gingerbread Caramel Trifle

Yield: 14–16 (6-ounce) jars

These trifle dessert jars are pretty simple to put together—technically, half of the recipe is store-bought. All you need to do is bake the cake, whip up the topping, and stuff the jars with this extraordinary flavor combination.

Ingredients

2 (16-ounce containers) caramel cream

2 (16-ounce) containers whipped topping, whipped

Gingerbread Cake

6 tablespoons margarine

½ cup sugar

¾ cup pure maple syrup

1 egg

2 cups Quality All-Purpose Cake Flour

1 teaspoon baking soda

1 teaspoon ground ginger

1 teaspoon cinnamon

¼ teaspoon salt

½ cup boiling water

Directions

Cake: Preheat oven to 350° F. Lightly grease a 9" square pan.

Using a mixer, beat the margarine with the sugar. Beat in the maple syrup and the egg. At low speed, beat in the flour, baking soda, ginger, cinnamon and salt. Add the boiling water and mix to incorporate. Pour the batter into the prepared pan.

Bake at 350° F for 35 to 40 minutes. Remove from oven and allow to cool. Once cooled completely, cut into 1" cubes.

Assemble: Distribute the gingerbread cubes among your jars or serving dishes. Layer the whipped cream and then top with the caramel.

Repeat the layers.

Note: These actually taste better after sitting overnight in the fridge.

E-Z Napoleons

Yield: 5 servings

A flaky sandwich filled with vanilla whip and berries—seriously, who wouldn't love that? This is one of those deliciously impressive dishes that makes it seem like I've worked really hard.

Prepare each of the components—the baked puff pastry squares, the cream, and the cut berries—in separate airtight containers, then assemble the Napoleons on Shabbos before serving, so they don't get soggy.

Ingredients

10 large puff pastry squares

1 (16-ounce) container whipped topping

½ (3.25 ounce) package vanilla instant pudding

10 fresh strawberries

1½ cups fresh blueberries

confectioners' sugar, as a garnish

mint leaves, as a garnish (optional)

Directions

Puff Pastry: Preheat oven to 400° F. Line a cookie sheet with parchment paper.

Place the squares of puff pastry squares on the lined cookie sheet and pierce the squares with a fork, forming holes in a few places so that the pastry doesn't puff up while baking.

Bake at 400° F for 8 to 10 minutes, or until golden and puffed. Remove from oven and allow to cool.

Store the baked puff pastry, layered with parchment paper, in a covered pan or container at room temperature.

Cream: Beat the whipped topping until stiff peaks form, then stir in half a package of vanilla instant pudding powder.

Store the cream in an airtight container in the refrigerator.

Tip: Instead of storing the cream in a container, place it in a Ziploc bag with the corner trimmed off. Place the bag in a drinking glass or container, and you have a piping bag all ready to go.

Berries: Clean the berries well, then pat dry and slice the strawberries thinly.

Refrigerate the cut berries in an airtight container lined with paper towel until needed.

Assemble: Place a generous spoonful of whipped cream on top of a square of puff pastry. Add the berries, then cover with another square of puff pastry on top, closing it like a sandwich. Sprinkle confectioners' sugar on top and garnish with mint leaves, if desired.

Chocolate Fondue

Yield: 2 servings

What's amazing about this recipe is that, although it's so easy to put together that it's hardly even a recipe, it looks so beautiful and presentable. It's loved by all—my children are always excited to have it, and Shabbos guests are always very impressed! This is definitely my go-to, because it literally requires almost no preparations. I just make sure to have good-quality dark chocolate on hand—and of course fresh fruit, which I usually have on hand anyway, as I buy fresh fruit *lekoved Shabbos.*

There are recipes out there for chocolate fondue, but I think all you need is just a good dark chocolate with a high percentage of cocoa. Don't worry that the chocolate will be bitter; it'll be coating super-sweet fruit. In addition to fresh fruit, you can add other fun stuff, either salty (like pretzels) or sweet (like marshmallows and lady fingers).

To melt the chocolate, I place the ramekins on top of a pan or pot (with food inside) on the hotplate, before the meal starts. With enough time, the chocolate will gently melt from the indirect heat.

Ingredients

2 (3.5 ounce) bars good-
   quality dark chocolate

12 strawberries

2 cups fresh pineapple, cubed

3 cups grapes

6 lady fingers

Mini skewers

Ramekins

Directions

Break the bar of chocolate into squares, put 3 to 4 squares in each ramekin, and place the ramekins somewhere warm, where the chocolate can melt.

Clean the fresh fruit well, cut the fruit into chunks, and thread them onto the skewers.

Arrange the fruit skewers and other items on large plates, place a ramekin of melted chocolate on the side of each plate, and serve immediately.

Note: This is the method I was told to use by my Dayan (Rabbi), but of course, everyone should consult their own Rabbi about this and any question of halachah.

Apple Custard Tarts

Yield: 2 large (14" x 4½") fluted tarts or 6–8 small (4½" x 2") fluted tarts

This is, hands down, the best apple tart I have ever had. This recipe is not one I would call easy, and although I would definitely put in my *"patchke"* file, I know I'll be pulling it out often … It's rich and decadent, the almond tart shell is nutty, yet subtle, and the filling is creamy and sweet.

Ingredients

Tart Shell

2 cups Quality All-Purpose Cake Flour

½ cup sugar

1½ sticks (12 Tablespoons) margarine

1 teaspoon salt

6 tablespoons water

1 cup sliced almonds

Custard Filling

1 (12-ounce) container Bakers Choice vanilla custard

2 eggs

2 teaspoons lemon juice

½ cup confectioners' sugar

Apples

3 Golden Delicious apples (or any firm apples), peeled, halved, and cored

1½ tablespoons brown sugar, for sprinkling

1½ teaspoons cinnamon, for sprinkling

Glaze

3 tablespoons apricot preserves

1 tablespoon water

Directions

Tart shell: Preheat oven to 350° F.

Place the flour, sugar, margarine, salt and almonds in a food processor fitted with the S-blade and pulse until blended. Gradually add in the water until the mixture forms a soft dough.

Press the dough into the bottom and sides of your fluted tart pans into a very thin crust.

Place the tart shells on a cookie sheet.

Bake the tart shells at 350° F for 11 minutes. Remove from oven and allow to cool slightly.

Custard filling: Using the food processor, beat the custard, eggs, lemon juice, and sugar

Note: For best results, use a fluted tart pan with a removable bottom. You can make these in mini personal versions, which are adorable, or as a large fluted tart, which is impressive as well.

together. Fill the cooled tart shells with the custard filling.

Apples: Cut each apple into 8 wedges, and then cut each wedge into three, so you have thin slices.

Arrange the apple slices over the custard filling.

In a small bowl combine the brown sugar and cinnamon. Sprinkle the apples with the mixture. (You won't use the whole amount.)

Bake and Glaze: Cut two large pieces of foil that together will fully cover the cookie sheet. Spray the foil with cooking spray and cover the entire cookie sheet with the foil (with the cooking spray facing the tarts).

Bake at 350° F for 30 minutes. Uncover and bake the small tarts for an additional 10 minutes, or the large tarts for an additional 15 minutes.

Remove from oven, uncover, and allow to cool on a rack.

Whisk the preserves and water in a bowl. Brush over the apples.

Creamsicle Layered Dessert

Yield: 2 (3–pound) loaf pans

This dessert is refreshing and sweet. I just love the combination of mango, orange, and vanilla—it's not just delicious; it's fruity and dreamy in a nostalgic sorta way…

Ingredients

32 ounces frozen mango, defrosted

2 cups orange juice

2 cups sugar

2½ tablespoons pure vanilla extract

24 ounces (1½ 16-ounce) containers whipped topping

1½ tablespoons vanilla sugar

Directions

Layer 1: Blend the thawed mango. Add in the orange juice, sugar, and vanilla and mix to combine.

Remove 2 cups of the mixture and set aside.

Divide the remaining mixture into 2 medium loaf pans and freeze for 2 hours.

Layer 2: Beat the whipped topping with the vanilla sugar until stiff. Remove 1½ cups of the mixture and set aside.

Pour the remaining mixture over the first layer and freeze for 1 hour, or until set.

Layer 3: Combine the reserved mixtures from layers 1 and 2. Spread over the second layer and freeze.

Serve frozen, cut into slices.

Fruit Tart Sandwich

Yield: 6 servings

In case you haven't yet noticed all the fruity desserts in this book—WE LOVE FRUIT! There's nothing as refreshing and purely sweet as fruit to complete a wonderful meal. This dessert was inspired by the classic fruit tart that once fell apart … This is how we improvised and made it even cooler!

Oh, and did I say "classic" fruit tart? Oh no, this is so much better, with a combination of the best components from the most mouth-watering tarts out there … The biscuits are buttery, and the cream is rich, thanks to the pareve cream cheese.

Ingredients

Biscuits

2 sticks margarine

5 tablespoons confectioners' sugar

2 teaspoons ground almonds

2 egg yolks

2¼ cups flour

Custard Cream

1 (16-ounce) container whipped topping

1 (8-ounce) container Tofutti pareve cream cheese

1 (12-ounce) package Bakers Choice vanilla custard

½ cup confectioners' sugar

Fruit Salsa

½ pomegranate, deseeded

4 strawberries, diced

½ mango, diced

1 kiwi, diced

4 teaspoons sugar

½ teaspoon lemon juice

Directions

Biscuits: Preheat oven to 320° F. Line a cookie sheet with parchment paper.

Using an electric mixer, beat the margarine and sugar together. Add the ground almonds, egg yolks, and flour, and mix well until combined.

Flour your working area well, as the dough is a bit sticky. Roll the dough out thinly and cut out a dozen 3½" to 4" circles with a metal cookie cutter. Transfer the circles to the prepared pan.

Bake at 320° F for 15 to 20 minutes, or until the biscuits are golden. Remove from oven and carefully transfer the biscuits to a cooling rack (they are very fine and soft, and can break easily).

Custard Cream: Using an electric mixer, whip the topping until stiff. Combine with the Tofutti cream cheese, vanilla custard, and confectioners' sugar and mix until smooth.

Fruit Salsa: Combine the fruits in a separate bowl and toss with the sugar and lemon juice.

Assemble: In the center of each plate, place a round biscuit. Top with about 3 tablespoons custard cream and 2 tablespoons fruit salsa (without the liquid). Place another round biscuit on top to form a sandwich.

Note: You will have extra custard cream. You can either halve the recipe, or do what I do—enjoy it to the last licks!

Creamy Custard Pareve Cheesecake

Yield: 1 (9") round cake

I developed this light, delectable recipe a few years ago, to introduce the incredible pareve Wayfare line that hit the shelves of our kosher market. This pareve cheesecake has a beautifully creamy consistency, and the custard gives it a unique and delicious flavor. Freezes well.

Ingredients

Crust

25 Vanilla sandwich cookies

3 tablespoons Wayfare pareve salted butter or margarine

Filling

3 (8-ounce) containers Wayfare pareve cream cheese, softened

1¼ cups sugar

1 cup Wayfare pareve sour cream

1 (12-ounce) package Bakers Choice Vanilla custard

2 extra large eggs

Decoration

Whipped topping (optional)

Vanilla sandwich cookies

Directions

Crust: Preheat oven to 350° F.

Using a food processor fitted with the S-blade, pulse 25 sandwich cookies to fine crumbs. Add the butter and pulse until combined. Press into an even layer on the bottom of a 9" springform pan.

Bake at 350° F for 10 minutes. Remove from oven and allow to cool as you prepare the filling. (I pop it into the fridge or freezer for 10 minutes.)

Filling: Using a mixer, beat the cream cheese and sugar until smooth. Add in the sour cream and the custard and mix well. Add the eggs, one at a time, and mix at low speed just until combined.

Pour the filling into the cooled crust. Place the pan in the oven.

Bake at 350° F for 50 to 60 minutes. Remove the pan carefully (the cheesecake may still be a little jiggly) and allow the cheesecake to rest until it is completely set. Then refrigerate for at least 4 hours or overnight.

Gently loosen the cheesecake from the sides of the springform pan, then open and remove the springform band.

Top with whipped cream if desired. Crumble the remaining sandwich cookies and sprinkle over the cheesecake. Serve chilled.

Chocolate Bark

Why I love chocolate bark:

#1 – It's chocolate, for goodness sake.

#2 – There are no rules. There are unlimited possibilities of delicious combinations you can create with the toppings. Think nuts, candy, raisins, crisp rice … The sky's the limit—and the sky is pretty high, if you know what I mean!

If you've never had chocolate bark, let me tell you what this craze is all about. It's just melted chocolate plus whatever crunchy goodies you fancy. It looks beautiful, in a scattered and organic sort of way.

These are two of my favorite variations, but remember that the recipes are merely outlines, and you can adjust toppings to suit your taste.

I like to serve Chocolate Bark on it's own, as a nosh—it's perfect for after the Shabbos meal, at the *butte* … But I sometimes incorporate the bark creatively into other desserts, too. For example, I often serve the Pomegranate Chocolate Bark on a plate with a scoop of vanilla ice cream, topped with a sweet pomegranate reduction.

Ingredients

10 ounces dark chocolate, chopped

Pomegranate variation

1 cup broken salted pretzels

¾ cup slivered almonds

¾ cup pomegranate seeds

Pistachio variation

1 cup shelled pistachios

¾ cup dried cranberries

Directions

Line a baking sheet with parchment paper.

Fill a small or 3-quart pot with water and bring to a boil.

Place the chopped chocolate in a Pyrex bowl. Place the bowl over the boiling water and allow the chocolate to melt. Once fully melted, stir in half the toppings.

Using a rubber spatula (or better yet, an offset spatula), spread the chocolate on the lined baking sheet until about ¼-inch thick, letting it

form whatever shape it takes naturally.

Top the surface of the chocolate with the remaining toppings. Refrigerate or freeze until the chocolate sets and hardens. Then crack in free-form style.

Store in an airtight container in the freezer.

Filbert Cream Cake

Yield: 40–50 individual square servings

Many of us who come from a Hungarian background have fond memories of specialty cream cakes, cut in square portions and served up in pretty paper cupcake holders at special occasions. My grandmother served many versions—this is one I remember fondly, and am so excited to share with the world! It's fluffy, nutty, and creamy—everything you wish for in a *heimishe* piece of homemade cream cake.

Ingredients

White Cake

6 eggs, separated

1½ cups sugar, divided

1 teaspoon vanilla sugar

¼ cup orange juice

1 tablespoon lemon juice

1¾ cups Quality All-Purpose
    Cake Flour

¼ cup oil

Nut Cake

6 eggs, separated

1½ cups sugar, divided

1 teaspoon vanilla sugar

½ cup oil

3 teaspoons cocoa

¾ cup ground filberts

¾ cup cup Quality All-
    Purpose Cake Flour

Chocolate Cream

4 eggs

3½ sticks (1¾ cups) margarine

1½ cups sugar

¾ cup cocoa

¼ cup water

3 teaspoons coffee

2 teaspoons vanilla sugar

Filberts, as a garnish

Directions

Preheat oven to 350° F.

White Cake: Using a mixer, beat the egg whites with ¾ cup sugar to form a snow.

In a separate bowl, mix the egg yolks with the remaining ¾ cup sugar and the rest of the ingredients. Gently fold the yolk mixture into the snow to form a smooth batter.

Line a baking sheet with parchment paper. Pour the batter onto the lined baking sheet. Bake at 350° F for 20 minutes.

Nut Cake: Using a mixer, beat the egg whites with ¾ cup sugar to form a snow.

In a separate bowl, mix the egg yolks with the remaining ¾ cup sugar, vanilla sugar, oil and cocoa. Gently fold the yolk mixture into the snow, then slowly add in the filberts and flour and mix to incorporate.

Line a baking sheet with parchment paper. Pour the batter onto the lined baking sheet. Bake at 350° F for 20 minutes.

Chocolate Cream: Using a mixer, mix the eggs and margarine until creamy.

Place the rest of the cream ingredients in a saucepan and cook for 5 minutes over medium heat, stirring constantly.

Remove from heat and allow to cool a bit.

Once cooled, add the cocoa mixture to the mixer with the eggs and margarine and mix well.

Transfer to an airtight container and refrigerate until it settles and becomes cream-textured.

Assemble: Place the white cake on your working area.

Cover with a layer of chocolate cream, then place the nut cake on top as a second layer.

Smear another layer of chocolate cream on top.

Cut the large two-layered cake into individual square portions.

Top each square with filbert nut, if desired.

Farbreinging • די באטע

A typical after-meal spread. We call it the *butte*, some call it the *oneg*, while others call it the *farbreing*. This extension of the Shabbos meal goes beyond the juicy fruit, sweet chocolate and savory nuts it features. It's a special time filled with yummy treats, beautiful singing and round-table discussions that foster feelings of togetherness. Every Shabbos I savor these fleeting moments of the *farbreinging*, spending time together solely for the sake of bonding and enjoying the company of one another. Dwelling in the exceptional hours of Shabbos, true *farbreinging* goes beyond the concept of time.

The primary way to instill the love of Shabbos in our children is by role modeling. When children see their parents enjoying Shabbos, it ignites their own enjoyment of Shabbos.

At the end of the day, when the meal is over, the family is still sitting around the table, basking in the Shabbos light. Shmoozing, eating, drinking and singing … relishing the coziness that's been created. The stars are shining brightly, reflecting the warmth that lingers long after the candles are out.

Baked Goods

The reason I and so many *balabustas* love Quality brand flour so much is because of its superior quality. No pun intended—I'm being super honest here.

Quality Flour is ground fresh weekly and rises beautifully, yielding fluffy and tasty results—whether you're baking challah or sponge cake.

I always use Quality High-Gluten Flour when baking things like bread, challah and babka. I can always tell the difference if I use another brand!

Quality All-Purpose Cake Flour: The result is perfect texture and fluffiness, no matter what I'm baking.

Quality Spelt Flour: When baking for people on special diets, this is a winner!

I use Quality Flour not only because of the results; its new, upgraded features have given me a whole new list of reasons I prefer this brand. Quality Flour traditionally comes in a brown paper bag, but now it also has a Pre-Sifted line packaged in super-practical plastic bags. It's a pleasure to save time on sifting, pour the Quality Flour straight out of the durable plastic bag, reseal its convenient Ziplock closure, and get amazing baking results. Every time.

Brown and White Cake

Yield: 1 tube pan

I knew I had to include a few good *"lekach"* recipes in my book, because that's what I'm always looking for. Rugelach and individual cookies are very nice, but sometimes what you want is a big pan of fluffy cake to serve the family. Here's one, and there's more where this came from…

Ingredients

7 eggs, separated

1¾ cups sugar, divided

2 cups Quality All-Purpose
   Cake Flour

2 teaspoons baking powder

¾ cup oil

¾ cup orange juice

2 tablespoons lemon juice

1 tablespoon vanilla sugar

1 tablespoon cocoa

¼ cup hot water

Directions

Preheat oven to 350° F.

Separate the eggs, placing the whites and yolks in 2 separate bowls.

Using a mixer, whip the egg whites together with ¾ cup sugar until stiff peaks form. Set aside.

In a separate bowl, mix the egg yolks with the remaining 1 cup sugar and add the rest of the ingredients (aside from the cocoa and hot water), one at a time. Gently fold the yolk mixture into the snow to combine well. Pour two-thirds of the batter into a tube pan.

Combine the cocoa and hot water. Mix the remaining one-third of the batter with the cocoa mixture. Pour the brown batter on top of the white batter.

Bake at 350° F for 1 hour, until a toothpick inserted in the center comes out clean.

Marble Cake

Yield: one 10" x 16" pan

This marble cake is light and fluffy, a good old-fashioned recipe that evokes only good memories…

Ingredients

13 large eggs, separated

1 cup sugar

1½ tablespoons vanilla sugar

1 cup orange juice

1 cup oil

3 cups Quality All-Purpose Cake Flour

3 teaspoons baking powder

¼ cup cocoa

3 tablespoons sugar

1 tablespoon vanilla sugar

Directions

Preheat oven to 350° F. Line a 10" x 16" pan with parchment paper.

Divide the egg yolks and egg whites in two separate bowls.

Using a mixer fitted with the balloon whisk attachment, whip together the egg whites and the sugar until stiff peaks form.

In another bowl, combine the egg yolks with the vanilla sugar, orange juice, oil, flour and baking powder.

Using a spatula, slowly fold the yolk mixture into the snow and combine.

Pour ¾ of the batter into the lined pan.

Mix the remaining ¼ of the batter with the cocoa, 3 tablespoons sugar, and 1 tablespoon vanilla sugar.

Dollop the cocoa batter onto the light batter in the pan, in several places.

Using a fork, lightly swirl the dark batter in a figure-8 motion to form a pretty marble design. Don't over-mix.

Bake at 350° F for 1 hour.

The Perfect Chocolate Cake

Yield: 1 (9" x 13") cake or 36 cupcakes

I share with you my go-to cake recipe. It's so easy: no need to separate, beat or whip; just mix the ingredients together—then bake! The results are wonderfully moist and fluffy!

Aside from this being the best chocolate cake I've ever tried, this recipe is also sort of sentimental to me and my extended family. My grandmother makes this cake in a round pan for every grandchild's birthday and decorates the cake with little candies forming the number of the child's age. She also bakes these cakes for my children, her great-grandchildren … She's never missed a birthday, despite the large number of grandchildren and great-grandchildren *kein ayin hure*, just like she never forgets to compliment, and makes me feel special whenever I see her.

Ingredients

6 eggs

1¾ cups water

1 cup oil

1 teaspoon vanilla sugar

3 cups Quality All-Purpose Cake Flour

2½ cups sugar

1 cup cocoa

1½ teaspoons baking powder

1⅓ teaspoons baking soda

Directions

Preheat oven to 350° F.

Mix all the ingredients, adding wet ingredients first and then dry ingredients slowly, one at a time until smooth and creamy, without lumps. Don't overmix.

Spray a 9" x 13" pan with baking spray or line with parchment paper.

Bake at 350° F for 1 hour and 10 minutes, until a toothpick inserted in the center comes out clean.

Note: This recipe is also great for baking cupcakes—just adjust the baking time to about 25 minutes.

Babbie's Fluffy Honey Cake

Yield: 3 (3-pound) loaf pans

My grandmother's fluffy, moist, and delicious honey cake. There's none like this one! Prepare your palate for the ultimate honey cake.

Ingredients

8 eggs

2 cups sugar

2 tablespoons vanilla sugar

1 cup oil

1 cup honey

1 cup water

1 tablespoon coffee dissolved in 1 tablespoon hot water

1 teaspoon cinnamon

4 teaspoons baking powder

4 cups Quality All-Purpose Cake Flour

Directions

Preheat oven to 350° F. Line three 3-pound loaf pans with parchment paper.

Using a stand mixer, beat the eggs together with the sugars. Slowly add the remaining ingredients, one at a time. Mix until the texture is smooth.

Pour the batter into the lined loaf pans.

Bake at 350° F for 50 to 60 minutes, until a toothpick inserted in the center comes out clean.

Vanilla Tea Cake

Yield: 1 Bundt cake

This cake was something I envisioned one day ... sometime in the middle of the night, I realized that I wanted a simple, yet tasty vanilla cake in my book—a staple that goes with everything. The tea was another brainstorm—it adds such a nice note, complimenting the vanilla flavor beautifully.

The result is a nice basic cake that's a real crowd-pleaser.

Ingredients

4 chamomile tea bags

1 cup hot water

6 eggs

2½ cups sugar

1 teaspoon baking powder

¾ teaspoon baking soda

1 (3.25 ounce) package instant vanilla pudding

1 tablespoon lemon juice

¾ cup oil

1 tablespoon pure vanilla extract

3 cups Quality All-Purpose Cake Flour

Directions

Pour 1 cup hot water over the 4 tea bags and allow to steep. Set aside until the tea is lukewarm.

Preheat oven to 350° F.

Using a mixer, beat the eggs with the sugar until the color is very pale yellow, almost white.

While mixing, slowly add the rest of the ingredients, one at a time, including the lukewarm tea. Mix until combined; do not over-mix.

Generously grease the Bundt pan with oil (use enough liquid oil, not a spray), then sprinkle with flour. Pour the batter into the prepared Bundt pan.

Bake at 350° F for about 1 hour, until a toothpick inserted in the center comes out clean.

Chocolate Rugelach

Yield: 48–60 rugelach

These rugelach are so soft and scrumptious! I like this recipe, because it's not huge, which makes it easier to whip up a batch of *heimishe* rugelach, and because the dough is incredible to work with.

Ingredients

Dough

4¾ cups Quality High-Gluten Flour

¼ cup sugar

½ teaspoon salt

½ tablespoon vanilla sugar

1 stick margarine

2 eggs

¼ cup oil

1 tablespoon dry yeast dissolved in 1 cup warm water

½ cup seltzer

Cocoa Filling

1¼ cups cocoa

2½ cups sugar

½ cup confectioners' sugar

¼ cup firmly packed brown sugar

Canola oil, for brushing dough

2–3 eggs, beaten, for brushing rugelach

Directions

To prepare the dough, mix all the ingredients (adding one at a time) in a mixer. Mix well for 10 minutes. If the dough is sticky, add more flour.

Cover and allow the dough to rise for 1 hour.

Preheat oven to 350° F. Line cookie sheets with parchment paper.

In a mixing bowl, combine the cocoa filling ingredients and mix well.

Divide the dough into 2 parts.

Roll out one section of dough into a large flat circle. (If the dough is sticky and hard to work with, keep adding small amounts of flour.)

Brush the thinly rolled dough with canola oil, then evenly spread a generous amount of cocoa filling over the surface.

Using a knife or pizza cutter, divide the dough into 8 "pizza-like" triangle-shaped segments, and then slice each triangle into 3 or 4 smaller segments. Roll each segment up (from the larger, outer edge inward) to form rugelach.

Place the rugelach on the lined cookie sheets and brush well with beaten egg.

Repeat with the remaining dough and filling.

Bake at 350° F for 25 to 30 minutes, until golden.

Note: This recipe can also be used to make 2 kokosh cakes—just increase the baking time to 45 minutes.

Chocolate Chip Brownies

Yield: 14–18 brownies

The perfect chocolate chip brownies, made easier (by eliminating the need to melt chocolate!) and made better by adding chocolate chips. I like to use good-quality dark chocolate chips for a rich, dense, *chocolatey* brownie.

Ingredients

2 cups sugar

2 sticks margarine

1¼ cups Quality All-Purpose Cake Flour

1 cup cocoa

5 eggs

1 tablespoon vanilla sugar

1 cup mini chocolate chips

Directions

Preheat oven to 350° F.

Using a stand mixer, beat the sugar and margarine. Add the rest of the ingredients and mix well.

Line a 9" x 13" pan with parchment paper. Pour the batter into the lined pan and spread into an even layer.

Bake at 350° F for 30 to 35 minutes.

Brownie Bars

Yield: 50–60 mini brownie bars

If you like Reisman's Brownie Bars, you won't like these. You'll love 'em! They have that melt-in-your-mouth dough and rich chocolate filling. Make them big or small —either way, you'll want to eat them all!

These were one of my favorite homemade treats growing up! I don't know where the recipe originates from, but it's been circulating, and for good reason.

Ingredients

Dough

5 cups Quality All-Purpose Cake Flour

4 sticks margarine

1 (16-ounce) whipped topping

Filling

1 cup flour

½ cup cocoa

1 (1-pound) box confectioner's sugar

3 tablespoons vanilla sugar

1 stick margarine

3 extra-large eggs

3 tablespoons oil

Dark chocolate, for drizzling

Directions

Preheat oven to 350° F. Line two baking sheets with parchment paper.

Using a mixer, prepare the dough by mixing the ingredients well until a smooth dough consistency is formed.

In a separate bowl, combine the filling ingredients and mix until well combined.

Divide the dough into 6 sections.

Spread a bit of flour over a clean working area and place the dough on it. Using a rolling pin, quickly roll a section of dough into a long, narrow rectangle, about ¼-inch thick (up to the length of your baking sheet).

Place one-sixth of the chocolate filling running down the center of the dough from top to bottom. Fold the two sides of the dough in. Place the roll onto the lined baking sheet, seam-side down.

Repeat with the remaining sections of dough and the rest of the filling.

Tip: To make cutting the bars easier, you can score the dough a bit before baking, creating marks to indicate where you'll want to cut.

Bake at 350° F for about 35 to 40 minutes. Do not over-bake; remove from oven while still pale—once they are golden, they will be too hard.

Cut into bars and drizzle with melted chocolate.

Candy-Studded Cookies

Yield: approximately 12 jumbo cookies

These cookies don't just look adorable, they're incredibly delicious, too. Super soft, loaded with sweet brown sugar zest! I absolutely love the chocolate lentils in there, not just because of how beautiful and studded they make 'em, but because they are so yummy! I mean, think of packets of candy-coated chocolate in every soft cookie bite.

This is the kind of recipe you'll make "for your children," and then end up eating most of them yourself ... Just saying. Loved by young and old, and the perfect Shabbos treat!

Ingredients

1 cup light brown sugar

¼ cup white sugar

2 tablespoons vanilla sugar

1 cup oil

2 eggs

2½ cups Quality All-Purpose Cake Flour

1 teaspoon baking soda

½ teaspoon salt

1 (7-ounce) container brightly colored chocolate lentils

Directions

Preheat oven to 350° F. Line a cookie sheet with parchment paper.

Beat the eggs and oil.

Add the remaining ingredients, aside from the chocolate lentils, and mix well.

With wet hands, form the dough into balls. Place the balls onto the lined cookie sheets and flatten into cookies.

Top each cookie with chocolate lentils, pressing them in a bit. (You can arrange a lot of the chocolate lentils close together, leaving way less space between one chocolate lentil and another than pictured ... they will spread out as the cookie grows.)

Bake at 350° F for 11 to 12 minutes.

Remove from oven and allow to cool completely on the cookie sheet. (Don't transfer the cookies immediately, or they'll fall apart.)

Bookie's Cheesecake

Yield: 1 (9") cheesecake (made in a springform pan)

This recipe is from my old neighbor Bookie, who we grew up with. Talk about a balabuste! My mother and I definitely gleaned a lot of kitchen-wisdom from her, and we are forever grateful. She gave this cheesecake every year for *mishloach manos*. That was the *mishloach manos* we most anticipated every year!

Personally, I don't like most cheesecakes—I find most of them to be too heavy and too sweet. Bookie's special recipe is our favorite. It's super-light and not overly sweet.

Ingredients

Crust

½ **pound Ostreicher's lemon cookies**

½ **stick (4 tablespoons) butter**

¼ **cup sugar**

Cheesecake

2 **tablespoons corn starch**

¾ **pound farmer cheese**

1 **(8-ounce) container J&J whipped cream cheese**

8 **ounces sour cream**

2 **eggs**

¾ **cup sugar**

1 **tablespoon vanilla sugar**

1 **cup milk**

Topping

8 **ounces sour cream**

1½ **tablespoons sugar**

1½ **teaspoons vanilla sugar**

Directions

Preheat oven to 350° F.

Combine the crust ingredients in a Ziploc bag or food processor, and mix until the mixture comes together. Press the mixture into a 9" springform pan to form the crust. Set aside.

Using a mixer, combine the cheesecake ingredients until the mixture has a smooth consistency. Pour the cheesecake batter over the crust.

Bake at 350° F for 1 hour. Remove from oven and allow to cool for 15 minutes.

Mix the topping ingredients together and smear on top of the cooled cheesecake. Decorate as you please.

Note: This recipe uses a 9" springform pan. If you skip the crust and use a readymade graham cracker crust, you will have enough extra cheesecake filling for an additional 4" x 6" pan.

Chocolate Roulade with Cheese Filling

Yield: 1 roulade

The ultimate nostalgic and show-stopping treat! The perfect soft cake, wrapped around a luscious filling, topped with a dairy chocolate glaze. After much testing and tweaking, I absolutely love this recipe, and have a feeling you will as well.

Ingredients

Chocolate Sheet Cake

5 eggs, separated

1 cup sugar

1 tablespoon vanilla sugar

1 cup Quality All-Purpose Cake Flour

½ teaspoon baking powder

4 tablespoons cocoa, sifted

2 tablespoons oil

¼ cup milk

Cheese Filling

½ cup vanilla Greek yogurt

1 (8-ounce) bar cream cheese, softened

1½ sticks unsalted butter, softened

1 cup confectioners' sugar

½ teaspoon pure vanilla extract

Chocolate Cream

1 (3.5-ounce) bar dairy chocolate (Schmerling's Swiss Milk)

1 stick butter, cut into pieces

2 egg yolks

½ cup confectioners' sugar

1 tablespoon cocoa

Directions

Bake the Cake: Preheat oven to 350° F.

Using a mixer, beat the egg whites, gradually adding the sugars, until peaks form. Add the egg yolks and the rest of the cake ingredients one by one. Mix until combined.

Line a 12" x 18" baking sheet with parchment paper. Pour the batter onto the baking sheet and spread evenly.

Bake at 350° F for 18 to 20 minutes, until a toothpick inserted in the center comes out clean.

Remove from oven and allow the cake to cool completely.

Flip the cake upside down onto a new sheet of parchment paper. Gently peel the used piece of parchment paper away from the top of the cake.

Starting from one edge, roll the cake up until it's completely rolled into the parchment paper, jelly-roll style. Refrigerate for at least 2 hours to set.

Prepare the Cheese Filling: Beat the filling ingredients together until smooth. Cover and refrigerate until set.

Assemble: Unroll the cake onto a sheet of foil.

Remove the cheese filling from the refrigerator and spread it evenly on the cake. Re-roll the cake, jelly-roll style and wrap it with foil. Refrigerate for at least 2 to 3 hours, until firm.

In a saucepan, combine the chocolate and butter. Cook over medium heat, stirring, until melted. Remove from heat. Add the remaining ingredients. Whisk well, until smooth.

Pour the cream over the fully set roulade. Refrigerate the roulade until set.

Shabbos Party

The Shabbos party is the highlight of Shabbos for children. Throw a party, prepare individual Shabbos *pekelach,* or allow the children to pick out a special nosh lekovod Shabbos. Whichever way you choose to celebrate doesn't really matter, as long as the spirit is there and the message is conveyed: Shabbos is sweet. Shabbos is our special treat.

Shalosh Seudos • שלש סעודות

Shalosh Suedos, the third meal that takes place right before sunset, is a very spiritual time. It is an *eis ratzon*, a special time for prayer and to receive additional blessing.

I like to keep *Shalosh Suedos* light. Along with the challah, I'll serve a vegetable salad or two and some fish spreads, such as white fish, lox and tuna.

Shalosh Suedos can sometimes be challenging, especially in the winter after a heavy Shabbos meal. But this is no reason to lose out on this heightened holy time and *mitzvah*. It's a time when we try to *chap arein*, to get just a little more Shabbos into our lives, before it slips away into another work week.

Melava Malka

"חמין במוצאי שבת מלוגמא"

The Gemara tells us that drinking or eating something warm on Motzei Shabbos is a segulah for healing. A warm bowl of nourishing soup is the perfect kind of comfort food to enjoy as we bid the Shabbos Queen goodbye…

Until next week.

The sky darkens. As the glimmering stars appear, I feel my soul constricting, a dull feeling overtaking my senses. The *neshamah yeseirah* has left together with the holy Shabbos. Although I know she will be back, right now all I can feel is that lumpy-heavy sensation swelling inside me.

I believe all *Yidden* feel sadness with the parting of Shabbos. It's difficult when the sweet Shabbos comes to an end, yet a *Yid* should not dwell in sadness. There are so many beautiful customs in the ritual of Havdalah to help uplift our mood. One of the reasons, according to Tosafos *(Beitzah 32)*, for smelling *besamim* at Havdalah is to lift the sadness caused when the neshamah yeseirah leaves us. Smelling the aromatic cloves helps lift the mood and calm the heart.

I've learned to take advantage of *Melava Malka,* which allows us to extend the experience of Shabbos as we escort the Shabbos Queen. It's another precious meal filled with fondness, Chassidishe stories, *zemiros* and warm food—an extension of the coziness of Shabbos.

Motzei Shabbos and *Melava Malka* are associated with such holy concepts: Eliyahu Hanavi, Dovid Hamelech and the Baal Shem Tov. The Orchos Chaim says that it is said in Kabbalah that Eliyahu Hanavi, who will come to notify us of the coming of Mashiach, will not come on Erev Shabbos or Erev Yom Tov, because *Yidden* are busy then preparing *lekovod Shabbos* and Yom Tov. But Eliyahu Hanavi will come on Motzei Shabbos, because of the *zechus* of Shabbos.

The *Melava Malka* dates back to the days of Dovid Hamelech, who begged Hashem to tell him when he would leave this world. Hashem refused, but He did reveal to Dovid that he would die on a Shabbos. Starting that week, Dovid Hamelech held a celebratory feast at the end of every Shabbos, thanking Hashem and reveling in the joy of being granted one more week of life.

I have such fond memories of *Melava Malka.* While my mother always prepared something warm to eat, my memories are primarily of the Chassidishe stories my father would tell us. I should probably mention that just as my mother is a great cook, my father is a captivating storyteller. The holy Rebbe Menachem Mendel M'riminov, zt"l, said that it's appropriate to remember the holy Baal Shem Tov at *Melava Malk*a and tell stories of his virtues, because it is a *segulah* for *hatzlachah* for the whole week in all areas—physically and emotionally.

Telling stories of the Baal Shem Tov and his students was a *minhag* my father took very seriously and never missed. Even when he had business travel and a Motzei Shabbos flight to catch, there was always a version of *Melava Malka,* washing for challah and a short story of the Baal Shem Tov involving an Ivan and a Kretchme. My siblings and I are all fluent in the names of the students of the Baal Shem Tov, and we know most of the popular stories. We each have our own favorite stories.

We light candles at the *Melava Malka* meal, which symbolically draws out the light of Shabbos into the rest of the week. Many people light two candles. Our family lights four, which is a segulah from the Baal Shem Tov. The Baal Shem Tov said that anyone who washes for a meal of *Melava Malka* and lights four candles every Motzei Shabbos is promised that he will not leave this world before seeing Dovid Hamelech, and will experience an everlasting salvation.

The Baal Shem Tov adds that if someone in the family is not well, or things are not going well, one should rejoice in the *Melava Malka* meal and say, "Ribono Shel Olam, may the merit of Dovid Hamelech benefit and protect me, that my request be fulfilled." It's promised that *Hashem Yisboroch* will help him when He sees how he fulfills the suedas melaveh malkah the best that he can, every week.

(קו' אמרי א"ש אות ב', מובא בס' חי וקים ברעזאן, מלוה מלכה דף צ')

Shabbos is fleeting. *Melava Malka* is a beautiful tradition which can be unique and comforting. The rituals, customs and devotion that make up our Shabbos and our *Yiddishkeit* are precious opportunities. It's for you to discover and connect to, in your own personal way, to infuse them with love, meaning, and joy.

Garlic Challah

Yield: 9 servings

Garlic bread is the perfect accompaniment to a warm bowl of soup at *Melava Malka* —and a great way to use your leftover challah!

Ingredients

9 thin slices challah

3 cloves garlic, crushed (fresh or frozen)

½ cup olive oil

parsley flakes (optional)

Directions

Preheat oven to 350° F.

Place the thin slices of challah on a baking sheet. Smear the challah with oil.

Place a bit of crushed garlic on each slice of challah and spread with a brush or spoon. Sprinkle with parsley flakes, if desired.

Bake uncovered at 350° F for 15 minutes.

Cauliflower Soup

Yield: 6–8 servings

This is my mother's delicious creamy cauliflower soup, which I like to serve garnished with garlic croutons or Veggie Sticks. For Motzei Shabbos, I often serve it with garlic challah.

Ingredients

½ cup oil

2 Spanish onions, chopped

2 (24-ounce) bags frozen cauliflower

1 knob celery root, peeled and cubed

8 cloves garlic

1½ tablespoons salt

freshly ground black pepper

6 cups water

1 (13.5-ounce) can coconut milk

Directions

Heat the oil in a large 6- or 8-quart pot over a high flame. Add the onions and sauté in oil until softened. Then add the rest of the vegetables and seasonings. Cook over medium-high heat for about 45 minutes, until the vegetables are soft.

Using an immersion blender, blend all the cooked contents of the soup. Once blended, add coconut milk until soup is creamy (up to 1 can).

Serve hot.

The RaizysCookin Hearty & Chunky Vegetable Soup

Yield: approximately 10–12 servings

I'm all for conveniences such as powders and frozen cubes of garlic and herbs, but when I can afford the time, I like to use fresh ingredients.

The key to a hearty and *"kreftig"* soup is a great base; it is the layering that builds rich flavor.

This is my go-to base—it's versatile and can be incorporated into many different soup recipes. You might be surprised about the little things that make such a difference. The fresh garlic. The fresh ginger (don't use dried). And last, but not least, the tomato sauce, which I always add to the base of soups, because a little tomato in the base adds an incredible depth of flavor.

Ingredients

Soup base

3 tablespoons canola oil

1 large Spanish onion, diced

4 cloves fresh garlic

2 tablespoons grated fresh ginger

8 ounces tomato sauce

Chunky Vegetables

8 carrots, peeled and chopped

7 yellow potatoes, peeled and chopped

4 large zucchini, chopped

3 parsnips, peeled and chopped

2 tablespoons kosher salt

freshly ground black pepper

3–4 tablespoons fresh parsley, chopped

Directions

Heat the oil in a large 8-quart pot. Add the onions and sauté for about 3 minutes over high heat. Reduce heat to medium-high, add the fresh garlic and sauté together with the onions for about 7 minutes.

Next add the grated ginger and tomato sauce and mix well.

Add all the chopped vegetables and seasonings, then fill the pot with water to cover. Cover the pot and bring to a boil. Cook over medium heat for about an hour.

Secret Tip: A great way to utilize leftover tomato dip from Shabbos is adding it to the base of a vegetable soup! Don't worry about how it's seasoned, it'll all add to the flavor of the soup.

Potato Zucchini Soup

Yield: 9 servings

A delicious, comforting bowl of soup.

Ingredients

6 yellow potatoes, peeled and cubed

1 (1-pound) bag carrots (about 9 small carrots), peeled and sliced into rings

4 large zucchini, peeled

water or chicken stock to cover

1 tablespoon onion soup mix

Salt and freshly ground black pepper

Directions

Place the cubed potatoes and sliced carrots in a large pot, and top with the 4 peeled zucchini. Fill the pot with water or chicken soup, so that the liquid is even with the top of the vegetables. Add the onion soup mix, salt and pepper. Bring to a boil, then reduce heat to medium-low and cook for at least 1 hour.

Transfer the zucchini to a separate bowl, and use an immersion blender to blend. Pour the puréed zucchini back into the soup pot and mix to incorporate.

Note: When making this soup for a fleishig dinner, I like to use chicken stock instead of water, for a deeper flavor.

Vegetable Bean Soup

⦀

Yield: 10–12 servings

This soup is healthy, wholesome, and super filling.

Ingredients

1 (16-ounce) bag great northern beans

1 (6-ounce) bag unseasoned split pea soup mix (or a combination of green and yellow split peas)

2 carrots

1 large parsnip

1 knob celery root

1 kohlrabi

3 zucchini, peeled and cubed

1 whole onion

3 cloves garlic, crushed

Salt and pepper, to taste

Directions

Fill a large 8-quart pot with water and bring to a boil. Add the great northern beans and split pea soup mix. Cover and cook at medium-low heat for 1 hour (or until the beans are cooked).

Meanwhile, using a food processor fitted with the "C" fine shredding blade, grate the carrots, parsnip, knob celery root, and kohlrabi.

After the beans have cooked for an hour, add in the grated veggies, cubed zucchini, and whole onion. Season with garlic, salt, and pepper. Cook over low heat for 1½ to 2 hours. Remove the onion before serving.

"The rituals, customs, and devotion that make up our Shabbos and our Yiddishkeit are precious opportunities. They are for you to discover and connect to, in your own personal way, to infuse them with love, meaning, and joy."

- Raizy Fried

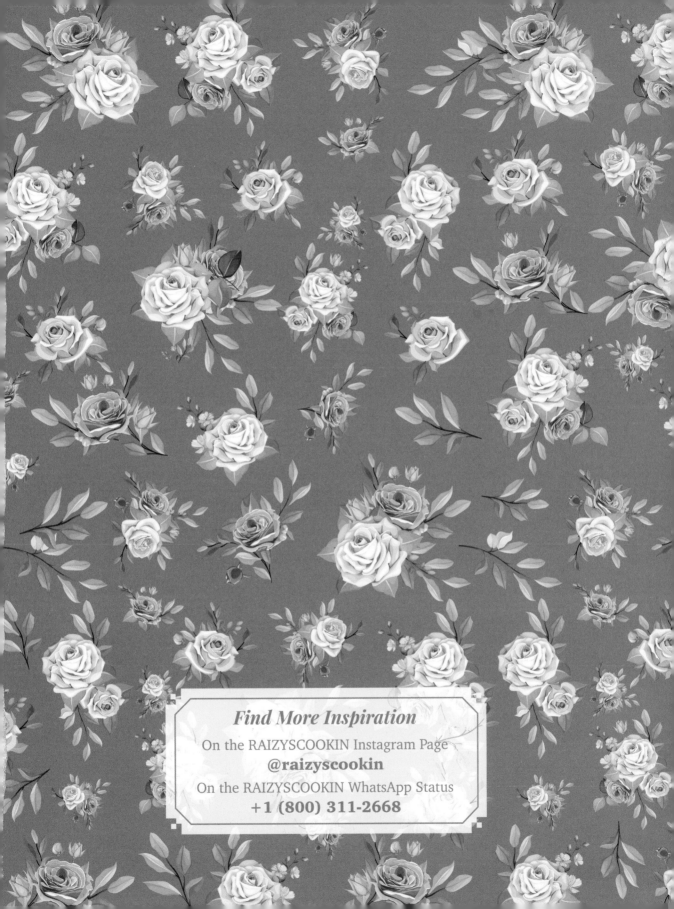